D1499935

Judy Blume

Other titles in the *Authors Teens Love* series:

Ray Bradbury
Master of Science Fiction and Fantasy
ISBN-13: 978-0-7660-2240-9
ISBN-10:   0-7660-2240-4

Orson Scott Card
Architect of Alternate Worlds
ISBN-13: 978-0-7660-2354-3
ISBN-10:   0-7660-2354-0

Robert Cormier
Author of The Chocolate War
ISBN-13: 978-0-7660-2719-0
ISBN-10:   0-7660-2719-8

Roald Dahl
Author of Charlie and the Chocolate Factory
ISBN-13: 978-0-7660-2353-6
ISBN-10:   0-7660-2353-2

Paula Danziger
Voice of Teen Troubles
ISBN-13: 978-0-7660-2444-1
ISBN-10:   0-7660-2444-X

S. E. Hinton
Author of The Outsiders
ISBN-13: 978-0-7660-2720-6
ISBN-10:   0-7660-2720-1

C. S. Lewis
Chronicler of Narnia
ISBN-13: 978-0-7660-2446-5
ISBN-10:   0-7660-2446-6

Lois Lowry
The Giver of Stories and Memories
ISBN-13: 978-0-7660-2722-0
ISBN-10:   0-7660-2722-8

Joan Lowery Nixon
Masterful Mystery Writer
ISBN-13: 978-0-7660-2194-5
ISBN-10:   0-7660-2194-7

Gary Paulsen
Voice of Adventure and Survival
ISBN-13: 978-0-7660-2721-3
ISBN-10:   0-7660-2721-X

Richard Peck
A Spellbinding Storyteller
ISBN-13: 978-0-7660-2723-7
ISBN-10:   0-7660-2723-6

Philip Pullman
Master of Fantasy
ISBN-13: 978-0-7660-2447-2
ISBN-10:   0-7660-2447-4

Jerry Spinelli
Master Teller of Teen Tales
ISBN-13: 978-0-7660-2718-3
ISBN-10:   0-7660-2718-X

R. L. Stine
Creator of Creepy and Spooky Stories
ISBN-13: 978-0-7660-2445-8
ISBN-10:   0-7660-2445-8

J. R. R. Tolkien
Master of Imaginary Worlds
ISBN-13: 978-0-7660-2246-1
ISBN-10:   0-7660-2246-3

E. B. White
Spinner of Webs and Tales
ISBN-13: 978-0-7660-2350-5
ISBN-10:   0-7660-2350-8

UTHORS TEENS LOVE

Judy Blume

Fearless Storyteller for Teens

Jen Jones

Enslow Publishers, Inc.
40 Industrial Road
Box 398
Berkeley Heights, NJ 07922
USA

http://www.enslow.com

Library of Congress Cataloging-in-Publication Data

Jones, Jen.
   Judy Blume : fearless storyteller for teens / Jen Jones.
      p. cm. — (Authors teens love)
   Summary: "A biography of author Judy Blume"—Provided by publisher.
   Includes bibliographical references and index.
   ISBN-13: 978-0-7660-2960-6
   ISBN-10: 0-7660-2960-3
   1. Blume, Judy—Juvenile literature. 2. Authors, American—20th century—Biography—Juvenile literature. 3. Children's stories—Authorship—Juvenile literature. I. Title.
   PS3552.L843Z74 2008
   813'.54—dc22
   [B]
                                                2007021493

Printed in the United States of America

10 9 8 7 6 5 4 3 2 1

Illustration Credits: Amanda Ruth Bakken, p. 10; AP/Wide World Photos, p. 6; Bridgepix.com, p. 14; Courtesy of Mary Ellen Janowski, Library Media Specialist, p. 25; Everett Collection, Inc., p. 27; Getty Images, p. 69; Marion Curtis/StarPix, p. 81; Robin Platzer, p. 78.

Cover Illustration: Debra Rohlfs (background); AP/Wide World Photos (inset).

Contents

Chapter 1

Anything But Ordinary

When Judy Sussman Blume was young, she aspired to be anything *but* a writer. A born-and-bred "Jersey girl," Judy found many ways to indulge her sizable imagination during her childhood. "When I was growing up, I dreamed about becoming a cowgirl, a detective, a spy, a great actress, or a ballerina. Not a dentist, like my father, or a home-maker, like my mother—and certainly not a writer, although I always loved to read," she has said.[1]

Though Judy did not discover her gift for writing until later in life, her love of storytelling shone through in her childhood hobbies. Paper dolls became lead actors in the elaborate plays Judy dreamed up. Costumes in the attic were transformed into wardrobe in Judy's pretend fea-ture films. While Judy practiced the piano, she entertained herself by giving lessons to imaginary students. She even kept a notebook with the names and progress of her pupils. "I always had an active imagination," Judy has said. "But I never wrote down any of my stories. And I never told anyone about them."[2]

Judy may have kept her tall tales a secret, but in seventh grade, her fantasy-filled world would expand to include a new friend. An Irish girl of great beauty, Mary Jane Sullivan proved to be just the creative companion Judy needed. After an initial meeting in homeroom, the pair were instantly inseparable. Sharing inside jokes and dreams of becoming actresses, Judy and Mary bonded over plays like *The Diary of Anne Frank* and movies such as *Rebel Without a Cause*. They idolized young Hollywood stars like Susan Strasberg and Natalie Wood.

After beginning studies at an all-girl high school, Judy and Mary wasted no time getting involved in extracurricular activities. Together they took modern dance classes and auditioned for drama club plays. Along with their love of art and performance, Judy and Mary found another way to channel their creative energies. The duo teamed up to coedit the high-school newspaper, *High Spots*. Judy soon discovered that she loved working with words.

Though the friendship remained strong throughout college, life intervened upon graduation. As each woman went her separate way, they found less time to spend together as they made room for husbands and children. Mary Sullivan became Mary Weaver, while Judy Sussman became Judy Blume. The stories Blume had stockpiled in her head as a child found their way to the printed page, as she embarked upon a highly successful writing career. As the years passed, the lifelong friends stayed in touch, but not as much as Blume would have liked.[3]

> ## The stories Blume had stockpiled in her head as a child found their way to the printed page.

Once Blume was an established author, she decided to pay tribute to their long-standing friendship. In 1993, she began work on *Summer Sisters*, a novel that was inspired by, and would later be dedicated to, Mary. At the center of the story were best friends who spent summers together on Martha's Vineyard while growing up. The book followed the intertwining lives of Caitlin, a beautiful, adventurous soul, and Vix, her caring, smart friend. Together the girls make an "NBO pact," in which they vow to never be ordinary. They believed that "to be ordinary was a fate worse than death."[4]

Just as Judy and Mary had, the characters of Caitlin and Vix inevitably grow apart as they grow up. Yet, like their real-life counterparts, Caitlin and Vix cling to their friendship through life milestones and tragedies. Writing the book was a labor of love for Blume, who considers Mary a "soulmate."[5] Though it is typical for Blume to rewrite a novel four or five times, she completed twenty drafts of *Summer Sisters* before it reached the final published version.[6] Though that may seem excessive, the revision phase is actually Blume's favorite part of the novel-writing process. "When I'm rewriting, I feel most creative," Blume has said. "I've got all the pieces to the puzzle, and now I get to put them together."[7]

Judy Blume greets fans and signs her best-selling books at the American Library Association Annual Conference in Chicago on June 25, 2005.

Because the subject matter was so close to Blume's heart, Blume was a nervous wreck when *Summer Sisters* was set for release in 1998. She was terrified that the book would fail. Panicked, she begged her husband, George Cooper, "You have to help me get this book back! We're going to give back the advance and we're going to stop this book. I've had a wonderful, long career and I don't want to go out this way."[8]

Though her past books had been hits with young adults and children, this was only Blume's third book targeted toward adults. To release some of her pent-up tension, Blume kept an "anxiety diary" as she prepared for a book publicity tour: "It's that time. The official pub date for *Summer Sisters* is tomorrow. I'm alternately thrilled and terrified—despondent and exhilarated. I go from thinking this is the worst book ever written to . . . I really like this book. I wonder how I did it?"[9]

Blume soon learned that she had worried needlessly. Readers enthusiastically embraced the book's theme of unconditional love between friends. They flocked in droves to *Summer Sisters*, making Blume's latest work her best-selling book to date. The book spent five months on *The New York Times* bestseller list, even reaching the coveted top spot.[10]

One look at Blume's list of accomplishments shows her own personal resolve to "never be ordinary." Over time, she has written twenty-four books, many of which paint a relentlessly honest picture of adolescence. Her frank and fearless storytelling style has attracted female fans of all ages around the world. (Blume's books have been translated into twenty languages and have sold more than 75 million copies.)

Though some of her children's books have come under fire for containing adult content, Blume is regarded as a pioneer in making it "okay" for teens to discuss their bodies and fears. Award-winning author An Na has remarked, "Thank God for Judy Blume or else I would have no clue about sex or the rest of my body. None of that got discussed at home, which I think is the case for so many other teenagers."[11] In further testament to her wide popularity, fourteen of her books reside on the *Publishers Weekly* list of the top 350 all-time best-selling children's paperbacks.[12]

Indeed, this ordinary girl from a middle-class New Jersey suburb has bloomed into an author with an extraordinary gift.

Chapter 2

Wartime Stories

On February 12, 1938, just two days before Valentine's Day, Judy Sussman was born to Randolph and Esther Sussman in Elizabeth, New Jersey. She was the second of two children, with her brother David four years her senior. Randolph, a dentist, and Esther, a housewife, had also been born and raised in Elizabeth, a middle-class suburb just outside of New York City.

Elizabeth held not only family significance but also historical significance as New Jersey's first capital (later replaced by Trenton in 1686). Originally known as Elizabethtown, the city was founded in 1664 by English settlers and became the first English-speaking community in the new colony.[1] Today, it serves as a bustling transportation hub, as home to parts of the Newark Liberty

<tr>

International Airport and the Port Newark-Elizabeth Marine Terminal. Also significant is the fact that well-known writers Philip Roth and Mickey Spillane also hail from nearby areas. "There must have been something in the water," Blume once joked.[2]

Somewhat of a "Daddy's girl," Judy developed an especially close relationship with her father during these early years. She spent hours in his basement workshop, watching him build odds and ends from scratch. "When I was small, he would sit me up on the workbench, with a hammer and nails so that I would feel included, and sharing something special with him," Judy remembers.[3]

Built in 1922, the Front Street Bridge is a historic landmark in Judy Blume's hometown of Elizabeth, New Jersey.

Not surprisingly, Judy's love of reading became quite evident at a young age. During preschool, she treasured a library-owned copy of *Madeline* by Ludwig Bemelmans. The book told the charming story of a little girl living in a French boarding school. "I didn't want to part with it. . . . I hid the book in my kitchen toy drawer so that my mother wouldn't be able to return it the library," Judy once told historian Leonard Marcus.[4]

Though life at the Sussman home was relatively peaceful, the outside world was embroiled in political and social turmoil. When Judy was a toddler, World War II began in the aftermath of Germany's invasion of Poland and Japan's attacks on China. Though the war primarily took place overseas, it affected Judy's young life as a self-proclaimed "child of suburbia."[5] Her mother and grandma often knitted olive-colored sweaters for the soldiers, and Judy's family gathered around the radio nightly, listening to news reports that both frightened and fascinated her.[6]

Judy's father Randolph took a position as a volunteer air-raid warden, fueling her already potent fears. His job was to patrol the city, enforcing "practice" blackouts and helping citizens prepare for possible enemy attack. Meanwhile, David took up plane spotting in the backyard and playing "soldier" while Judy chose to play with her dolls.[7]

Along with its safety implications, the war resonated on an intensely personal level with the Jewish Sussmans. In what became a very vivid memory for Judy, she and her family once went to the Bronx to visit a relative who had narrowly escaped the horrors of a German concentration camp. "[He] had survived the Holocaust by 'living in a hole,' as I was told. I began to wonder about this. *How could he have lived in a hole? What kind of hole was it? How did he eat and sleep and go to*

the bathroom in a hole? Was there a series of holes
in which people lived?" remembers Judy. "It was
one of those things that a young child couldn't
possibly understand, even though I knew it was all
very serious and grim and had to do with being
a Jew."[8]

When the war came to a close in 1945, Judy's
family was vacationing in Bradley Beach, New
Jersey. Seven-year-old Judy was eating a jelly sand-
wich and listening to Bing Crosby with her mother
and grandma. What began as an ordinary lunch soon
transformed into an unforgettable moment in time.
After an announcer interrupted the broadcast to
proclaim the war had ended, Judy and her family
chanted and danced around the boardinghouse
kitchen, soon joined by other gleeful vacationers.[9]

This celebration is mirrored in *Starring Sally J.
Freedman as Herself*, which Judy calls her most
autobiographical work. In the book, young Sally
rejoices with her family after learning about the
war's conclusion: "So now Daddy wouldn't patrol
the streets anymore, wearing his white air raid
helmet. And she and Douglas wouldn't get into
bed with Mom, waiting for Daddy to come home,
telling them it had just been practice, that the war was
far, far away, and nothing bad was ever going to hap-
pen to them."[10]

> "It was one of those things that a young child couldn't possibly understand."
>
> —Judy Blume

Set in 1947, the book explored the main character Sally's fantasies, fears, and adventures while adjusting to the postwar climate in Miami Beach, Florida. Convinced Adolf Hitler is alive and living nearby under an alias, Sally writes letters to him. "Sally's world is the world as I perceived it at age 10. A world of secrets kept from children, a world of questions without answers," Judy has said.[11] And, like Sally, Judy had coped with the realities of war by escaping to the safety of her pretend world: "I always had an active fantasy life, fueled by the movies. Following World War II, I fantasized about being a hero myself—a member of the Underground, fighting Hitler."[12]

As Judy entered third grade, her brother David became seriously ill with a kidney infection. At the recommendation of the family doctor, the family relocated from Elizabeth to Miami Beach. Their hope was that the warmer climate would bring about a quick recovery. To Judy's dismay, her father stayed behind to run his dental practice. Though he visited once a month, Judy missed him terribly.[13]

Being so far from her father not only separated Judy from her closest confidant, but it also exacerbated her fears about his health. Two of Randolph's brothers had died in their early forties, and Judy was convinced that her father awaited a similar fate. Judy's fixation with death had deep roots. Not only had both uncles passed away at a relatively young age, but her aunt and grandmother had also died by the time Judy was ten years old. During a 2005 interview with *Instructor* magazine, Blume shared that "death [was an experience that shaped me]. We were always 'sitting shivah.'"[14] (Shivah is a Jewish tradition created to honor the dead, in which surviving family members spend seven days in mourning.)

Complicating matters was the fact that the Sussmans' first year in Florida coincided with Randolph's forty-second birthday. Judy spent a great deal of time worrying about what appeared to be a family curse. After all, both of her uncles had died at that age. Though she kept her fears private from others, Judy says she "became ritualistic, inventing prayers that had to be repeated seven times a day, in order to keep [her] father safe and healthy."[15]

Even without her father there, Judy found herself in quarters almost too close for comfort with the rest of her family. They had taken up residence in "a tiny apartment in a pink stucco building with a goldfish pond in the courtyard."[16] Judy and her brother slept on daybeds in the living room, while her mother and grandma shared a bed in the alcove. Yet Judy did not let the cramped quarters dampen her spirits. In fact, she credits her time spent in Miami Beach with helping her come out of her admittedly shy shell. When not attending Central Beach Elementary School, Judy spent a great deal of time playing at the beach, taking ballet classes, and roller-skating to music in Flamingo Park.[17] She even teamed up with her friends to stage a ballet show benefiting a Jewish charity.[18]

Judy regards the two school years she spent with her family in Florida as the "most memorable years" of her early life.[19] As such, the plot of *Starring* . . . displays many striking parallels to Blume's own childhood, with Sally's family moving to Miami Beach to care for her sickly brother, Douglas. Their dentist father stays behind, and Sally is consumed with worry about his well-being. References to Jewish traditions and her grandmother's colorful Yiddish expressions are also included.

> ## "Death [shaped me]. We were always 'sitting shivah.'"
> ### —Judy Blume

From the turbulent times of war to the colorful confines of Florida living, Judy found plenty of fuel for her endless imagination. One of her favorite pastimes was to spend countless hours bouncing a pink Spalding ball against the side of her house.[20] As she did so, Judy would make up dramatic story lines inside her head about glamorous movie stars or girl detectives. "[As I bounced the ball], the stories would just come," Blume said during a National Public Radio interview in 2004. "I was always inventing stories inside my head that I never shared. It felt weird having them there."[21]

The sheer volume of her daydreams was matched only by the number of books she read. Though Judy's tastes varied, she found herself especially drawn to books with female protagonists, such as the *Nancy Drew* books by Carolyn Keene and the *Betsy-Tacy* series by Maud Hart Lovelace. "I loved the characters [in *Betsy-Tacy*]; they were alive for me," Judy has said. "Betsy's family life seemed so wonderful, with their lively Sunday suppers and huge family gatherings."[22]

A hearty love of reading ran in Judy's own family. Her parents had an extensive book collection, while her aunt Frances (a grade-school principal whom Judy affectionately called Fanta) also boasted an impressive array of immaculately kept classics.[23] A regular customer at the local Ritz bookstore, Judy bought one new book per week with her allowance.[24] Today, Blume remembers many a day spent "sitting on the floor at the Elizabeth Public Library . . . not just turning the pages and pouring over the pictures, but sniffing the books. I loved the way they smelled, like a warm, ripe *blankey*."[25] Little did she know that one day her own work would sit on those very same shelves.

Chapter 3

Little Dreams, Big Talent

Over the last thirty-plus years, Blume's books have struck a universal chord with children and young adults. Blume credits this phenomenon to her unique ability of authentically capturing their point of view. Blume says today, "I am still 12 years old inside. . . . As I grow older, I split in half because I see myself as the woman, the mother, the grandmother that I am, and I also can put myself back and identify totally with children."[1]

One of the reasons Blume is so in touch with young adulthood is that this time in her own life was one of tremendous transformation. Not only was her body changing, but her personality and perspective were taking new shapes as well. No longer was Judy the shy, quiet girl she had been until the fourth grade. She was now an outgoing preteen more brazen about exploring her curiosities and overcoming her fears.

In her book, *Otherwise Known as Sheila the Great*, Judy conveys the trials and triumphs of facing childhood fears—from dogs to thunderstorms to the dark.[2] The main character, Sheila Tubman, spends a life-changing summer in Tarrytown, New York. Through new experiences, Sheila is forced to drop her brave front and admit her shortcomings. Like Sheila, Judy had always been terrified of dogs. In fact, she enlisted her friend Barry to walk her the two blocks to school every day as protection from neighborhood pets.[3]

To Judy's dismay, her brother, David, was successful in convincing their parents to get a family dog. Yet the fates stepped in on Judy's behalf. The Sussmans' first dog, Skippy, ran away. Their second dog, Teddy, had a serious problem with car

---

No longer was Judy the shy, quiet girl she had been until the fourth grade.

---

sickness and had to be returned to his first owner's farm.[4] It was not until much later in life, when Blume's grown son adopted a dog, Mookie, that Judy came to see dogs as four-legged friends.

Learning to swim was another major obstacle

that Judy overcame with time. While living in Miami Beach, David often teased her for pretending to swim by keeping one foot on the bottom and moving her arms.[5] It was not until Judy spent a summer at Camp Kenwood in Connecticut that she finally learned to love the water. Though it seemed like an impossible feat, Judy passed her "blue cap" test by swimming four laps across the lake.[6] She chronicled this achievement in *Sheila the Great*: "Marty was wrong. The pool wasn't forty feet across. It was really forty miles. I never should have tried it. . . . Then my hand touched the ladder. . . . Marty was yelling, 'You made it! You made it! I knew you would!' It was true. I swam across the deep end of the pool and I was still alive! I really and truly did it!"[7]

Like many of her characters, Judy was a "late bloomer." Strikingly thin and self-conscious about it, Judy had always resented her weight. She longed to be picked first for the kickball team, but was passed over time and again for sturdier classmates. She dreaded the weekly weigh-in with the school nurse, who would announce, "Not quite fifty [pounds] yet." Remembers Judy, "Thin was not 'in' when I was growing up. The boys teased me, saying, 'If Judy swallowed an olive, she'd look pregnant.'"[8]

The Sussman family's permanent return to New Jersey from Florida coincided with Judy's entering the fifth grade. David had regained his health, and the family would no longer be separated during the school year. As she reconnected with old friends, Judy found that many had passed into the throes of puberty. She secretly envied those who seemed to be developing more quickly than she was. On her Web site, she admits to stuffing her bra, lying about getting her period, and doing "bust-enhancement" exercises in an effort to catch up.[9] These insecurities later played a major role in the plotline for *Are You There, God? It's Me, Margaret*.

In sixth grade, Judy and four of her friends formed a club they dubbed the "Pre-Teen Kittens."[10] At their frequent sleepovers and after-school meetings, the girls giggled and gossiped about boys. They excitedly whispered predictions about who would be the first to get her period. To them, menstruation was a mystery, and Judy was dying to uncover the secrets behind it. She had asked her father about it once, but he had given a confusing answer about the moon's cycle.[11] Books were not much help either. Judy had looked up "sex" in the *World Book Encyclopedia* only to find descriptions of reproduction in plants. Blume later said, "If someone had just told me the truth, my curiosity would have been satisfied. I wanted to know about the grown-up world."[12]

Along with the stresses of keeping up physically with her peers, Judy felt pressure from her family to be "perfect." In many ways, she felt as if she had grown up in David's shadow. Yet she also saw what she perceived as her parents' disappointment in him.[13] David had shown great promise, beginning his schooling a year early. Regarded as a genius by some, David often retreated to his dad's basement workshop, where he built his own radio and oscilloscope. Yet he was somewhat of a loner and earned poor grades.[14] "David wasn't a parent pleaser, so that role fell to me," Blume once said.[15]

In light of David's falling short of expectations, Judy made every effort to exceed them. Her quest for perfection led her to become what some might call a textbook overachiever. She excelled in school, earning good marks. When she entered all-girl Battin High School, Judy was outgoing and motivated. She wasted no time getting involved

Battin High School was once the only all-girl public high school in the United States. Today, the building serves as a co-ed, public middle school.

in many extracurricular activities, such as choir, modern dance, the school newspaper, *High Spots*, and drama club. Though Judy had many friends, she often felt the need to paint a rosy picture when asked about school parties and dances: "When I look back now and think of the times I lied to my mother to please her, to assure her that yes, indeed, I was the most popular, best all round girl, I cringe. I kept my anxieties to myself."[16]

High school was the time that Judy decided to chase her childhood dream of becoming an actress. She and best friend Mary Sullivan often made the trek into Manhattan to check out the newest plays—now it was their turn to shine! In tenth grade, Judy and Mary earned parts in the school production of *Stage Door*, which famed stage actress Phyllis Kirk had starred in during her days at Battin. On a visit to her alma mater, Kirk stopped into a cast rehearsal to lend support and give advice. Mary and Judy were shocked and thrilled—they had never seen one of their stage idols up close and personal![17]

Yet despite all the exposure, acting began to seem less like an attainable goal. Says Blume, "My father's dreams for me were a lot like my own. He saw me on the stage and would have taken me to the best acting teachers. But by the time I was fourteen, I was identifying more with the reality that I would probably become a mother and wife, maybe president of the PTA. This *was* the fifties, after all."[18]

Though Judy was a model student, she felt

A 1950s publicity photo of Phyllis Kirk. Kirk was best
known for her work in the film *House of Wax* (1953)
and the television program *The Thin Man*. A graduate of
Battin High School, she returned to visit the school and
met Judy Blume while Blume was still a student there.

stifled in many of her classes. Just a handful of her teachers introduced what Judy felt to be challenging material, and even fewer "encouraged us to think for ourselves, which I consider the most important part of any education," Blume later said.[19] Yet it was no surprise to anyone when Judy graduated at the top of her class in 1956. Her parting yearbook quote read: "Keep a place within your heart for little dreams to go."[20]

At the Battin graduation ceremony, Judy and Mary looked eagerly toward the future. They had skipped out on senior prom to attend June Week at the Naval Academy in Annapolis, Maryland, and had an unforgettable time flirting with the cadets and flitting about campus together. Now the best friends sat next to each other (thanks to the proximity of their last names—Sullivan and Sussman) in caps and gowns, anticipating their next moves. Judy was off to Boston University to study elementary education; Mary was to pursue acting at the American Academy of Dramatic Arts.[21]

Looking back, Blume remembers high school fondly, but takes time to examine the influences that shaped her teenage self: "Oh, I'm not that crazy about the teenager I was. I much prefer the interesting person I was (to me, anyway) before I was a teen. . . . As a ten year old, I had a depth and curiosity that still interests me. Maybe that happens to all of us. We're too into being like everyone else. Too concerned about how we look to our peers when we're teens."[22]

That September, Judy headed for Boston

University, where she was to room with two other freshman girls in Charlesgate Hall. Though she felt as if she should enjoy her newfound freedom, Judy instead felt tired and rundown. The day before leaving for a three-day orientation trip, Judy collapsed in her dorm room.[23] Tests later showed that she had contracted a serious case of mononucleosis. It soon became apparent that Judy would not be able to finish out the semester, and she headed home to New Jersey.

Judy's bout with "mono" was the first of many illnesses that plagued her throughout her twenties. Today, Blume wonders if her physical ailments were a direct result of depression: "I had one exotic illness after another. No one said, 'Maybe she needs Prozac.' Back then, we couldn't admit we were unhappy. We couldn't admit anything less than perfection."[24] Blume did not achieve better health until her thirties, when she began her writing endeavors. Later in life, Blume would credit writing as a means of catharsis—her way of releasing negative energies that had affected her well-being.

But first, it was off to New York University, where a fresh start and a new path beckoned to the Boston University transfer.

Chapter 4

From Dishes to "Dr. Suss"

Judy Sussman Blume has been quoted as saying she went to college to accomplish two things: becoming an elementary school teacher and finding a husband.[1] Though Judy's first aspiration was not to be, her romantic goal did not take long to materialize. It was during her sophomore year at New York University that Judy met her future spouse. Over the holiday break, Judy traveled home to see her parents, who had relocated from Elizabeth to Westfield, New Jersey. One night, she attended a party in her parents' neighborhood, where she met a twenty-five-year-old lawyer named John Blume.[2]

For the next year, Judy and John engaged in a whirlwind courtship. Happy and in love, Judy was enjoying all that college and Manhattan had to offer. She loved talking politics and art with the resident beatniks, and she often dressed the part in black turtlenecks and corduroys.[3] "[My friends and I] walked around the Village and pretended to be very bohemian," Judy once told interviewer Betsy Lee.[4] Yet Judy's parent-pleasing tendencies had not completely disappeared. On her visits home, her wardrobe reverted back to the sensible sweater and skirt sets from her high-school days.[5]

In December 1958, about one year after the couple first met, John proposed marriage.[6] An elated Judy said, "Yes!" The wedding was slated for August 15, 1959, at the Hampshire House overlooking Central Park in New York City.[7] Time passed quickly as Judy continued her junior year and excitedly made plans for the big day. She was especially thrilled that David, who had been stationed overseas for four years, would return from Libya in time for the wedding.

One Sunday afternoon in July 1959, Judy and her parents drove to the Newark airport to pick up David and his wife. In light of the approaching wedding, good news seemed abundant as David announced that he and his wife were expecting their first child. Randolph heartily exclaimed, "What a banner year for our family!"[8] Yet after returning to the Sussman home in Westfield, Randolph lay down on the couch and told Judy that he felt "strange." Judy nervously held his hand as they waited for the doctor to arrive. Sadly, there was no saving Randolph. Blume's worst childhood fears were realized—a heart attack had claimed her father's life.[9]

As she processed the terrible turn of events, Judy's mind flashed through her treasured history with her father—their special game of hide-and-seek when she was young, the recreation room he had lovingly built for their family, the records they had listened to together every night in the parlor.[10] She reminisced about his upbeat personality and his encouragement of her hopes and dreams. Suddenly, her future looked dim without her father around to be part of it.

Though it was difficult to move forward with the wedding as planned, Judy and John were bound by Jewish tradition to proceed. According to Judaism beliefs, a wedding must not be cancelled during a time of mourning.[11] The couple chose to forego the Hampshire House event for a much smaller ceremony at the Sussman home on August 15, 1959. It was a bittersweet affair as the family struggled to make sense of the tragedy that had taken place just weeks earlier. Mary Sullivan was on hand to support Judy, who credits her today with helping her through this extremely emotional time.[12]

Walking down the aisle, Blume tried to adapt

> **Blume's worst childhood fears were realized—a heart attack had claimed her father's life.**

her father's positive outlook. "It was not a weepy wedding. My father was such a jolly, loving, philosophical person, and everyone knew that he would insist that it go on and that we smile. And we did," Blume told writer Maryann Weidt.[13]

As Blume entered her senior year of college that fall, more major life changes lie in store. No sooner had she and John adjusted to the rhythms of married life than Blume learned that she was pregnant. In the spring of 1961, Blume received her degree in elementary education. Later that year, Randy Lee Blume was born. Though she had originally planned to take a teaching job upon graduation, Blume chose instead to stay home with young Randy and assume housewife duties.

Two years later, the Blumes were immersed in suburban New Jersey life. Shortly after relocating from Plainfield to Scotch Plains, the couple's second child, Lawrence Andrew Blume, was born in 1963. Though Blume loved taking care of her children, she began to feel lonely and a bit restless. She and Mary had grown apart over time, and Blume missed having women her own age to confide in. Attempts to make friends in her neighborhood proved fruitless, as Blume shares on her Web site: "I was constantly hoping to find someone with whom I could connect. Each time a moving van brought a new family to our cul-de-sac, I'd be out there, a welcome committee of one, hoping this would be it. It never was."[14]

Slowly but surely, Blume began to reawaken her creative energies as a way of escaping the suburban blues. Coupling her teaching background with her newfound parental wisdom, Blume set to work making decorative felt banners for children. Her new hobby was met with relative success when Bloomingdale's placed an order for her creations.[15] There was no doubt about it—Blume knew how to connect with kids.

Each night while doing the dishes, Blume found herself concocting rhyming stories, much like the picture books she often read to young Randy and Larry. She envisioned herself a famous author like Dr. Seuss. "My maiden name was Sussman, so I thought I could at least be the next Dr. Suss," Blume once joked on National Public Radio.[16] In hopes of getting published, Blume turned her dinnertime musings into picture books. She even illustrated them using colored pencils, which she now laughs about: "I'm totally not an illustrator, so it was sort of a joke. . . . [I] fastened them with little brass fasteners like I was still in school."[17]

One day, Blume received a brochure from New York University (NYU) in the mail. Inside was an advertisement for an adult education class on "Writing for Children and Teenagers." Having submitted some of her amateur picture books to publishers with no luck, Blume considered the brochure a sign to keep trying.[18] She wasted no time enrolling in the class. Each Monday, Blume took a bus into the city while John took the kids out for dinner.[19]

The instructor, author Lee Wyndham, proved to be an inspiring force and very supportive of

Blume's early efforts. "She wrote me little notes telling me I would get published one day," Judy has said.[20] Wyndham's encouragement provided just the push Blume needed as the rejection letters had continued to pour in. One from *Highlights* magazine read, "Does not win in competition with others."[21] Another author told her, "Give it up; you have no talent."[22] Blume enjoyed the class so much she decided to take it all over again, her drive renewed and her confidence slowly gaining.

> # Wyndham's encouragement provided just the push Blume needed.

Blume's second go-round at the writing class provided the genesis for what would later become *Iggie's House*. Each week, she wrote one chapter and turned it in to Wyndham, who would give valuable guidance and feedback. In the meantime, Blume began to spend a great deal of time at the library. She checked out books like *Jennifer, Hecate, MacBeth, William McKinley, and Me, Elizabeth* by E. L. Konigsburg and *Harriet the Spy* by Louise Fitzhugh. "In the beginning, I would . . . bring home stacks of books and I'd divide them into piles—'these are books I really love' and 'I'd like to write this way.' I used to laugh so hard reading [Beverly Cleary's] books I'd fall off the sofa," Blume remembers today.[23]

In 1966, Blume received her first piece of good news. Two of her short stories, "The Flying Munchkins" and "The Ooh Ooh Aah Aah Bird," had been accepted for publication.[24] Blume was paid twenty dollars for each submission,[25] and Wyndham presented her with a congratulatory red rose in class.[26] Throughout the year, Blume's hard work in the class continued to pay off, as *Trailblazer* magazine later ran *Iggie's House* in serial form.

Finally, Blume felt validated. The emptiness she had felt inside had been replaced by a strong sense of fulfillment. During a 2004 acceptance speech, Blume said:

> I adored my children but inside was an empty space, a gnawing, an ache that I couldn't identify, one that I didn't understand. The imaginative, creative child grows up and finds that real life, no matter how sweet, is missing some essential ingredient. . . . Once I started to write, my illnesses magically disappeared. I found an outlet for all that emotion, all that angst. Writing saved my life and it changed it forever.[27]

Blume finally got her first "big break" at the age of thirty-one. One of the picture books she had written several years back was about to see the light of day. Reilly and Lee was set to publish *The One in the Middle Is the Green Kangaroo*, about a middle child finding his own special place in the family. In the fall of 1969, it became Blume's very first published book. Blume was beyond thrilled. She devoured the first copy, sniffing the pages just as she had when she was young.[28]

At her first book signing in Scotch Plains,

Blume realized it would be a long road to the top. Other than Esther, Randy, and Larry, just a handful of friends showed up. Remembers Blume, "I sat there for a couple hours next to a stack of books hoping, praying someone I wasn't related to would walk through that door. But no one did."[29]

Still riding high on her recent successes, Blume came upon a listing from a new publisher in *Writer's Digest*. Bradbury Press was seeking "realistic fiction for the eight-to-twelve set."[30] Blume could not help but think of *Iggie's House*. An early version had run in *Trailblazer*, so she knew the book had promise. Why not? Blume thought as she sent the book for consideration. Soon Blume was called in for a meeting with Richard Jackson, an editor at Bradbury. Though some revisions would be necessary, Jackson believed the project could be a viable and relevant one. (Later in life, he would call the ad placed in *Writer's Digest* "the best $5,000 we ever spent."[31])

Centering on the racial tensions of the 1960s, *Iggie's House* is the tale of Winnie Barringer, a spunky young white girl who befriends the only black family in her neighborhood. As one excerpt reads:

> Glenn read the sign in a hoarse and whispery voice, as if he needed to say it out loud to believe that it was real. GO BACK WHERE YOU BELONG. WE DON'T WANT YOUR KIND AROUND HERE! Mr. Garber grabbed the sign, yanked it out of the ground and broke it in half over his knee. Winnie felt her cheeks burning. She was shaking all over. "We're not all like that," she heard a small voice say. "We're not . . . we're not . . . we're not." She realized the

voice was her own and that she was crying. She turned and fled, tears streaming down her face.[32]

Bradbury Press published the book in 1970, and Blume dedicated it to Lee Wyndham. Blume felt incredible lucky to have Wyndham and Jackson as early champions of her work. Today Blume says, "Once I met Dick Jackson, everything fell into place. It was like *Sleeping Beauty*: I had awakened, and from that time on, I wrote one book or more per year."[33]

Indeed, in going from unhappy housewife to up-and-coming author, Blume was about to experience her own Cinderella story.

Chapter 5

A Writing Star Is Born

As Blume entered her early thirties, her writing was becoming more of a profession than a pastime. She had encountered some success with her early efforts, but Blume felt there was still a large amount of material brewing beneath the surface. For her next book, Blume decided she would write from deep within and see what came out.

Though now a grown woman with children of her own, Blume still felt closely in touch with the curious, confused girl she once was. She remembered how it felt to seek answers in books and find none to which she could relate. Around age twelve, Judy had raided her parents' bookshelves and pored over books by J. D. Salinger and the Brontë sisters.[1] Yet she had been unable to find anything about puberty's rites of passage.

Refusing to let another generation wonder and worry about their changing bodies, Blume set to work on *Are You There, God? It's Me, Margaret*. The book follows the coming-of-age of a young girl named Margaret Simon. Readers follow Margaret as she experiences important life milestones like her first period, first kiss, first bra, and first party. In the book, Margaret joins a secret club inspired by Blume's childhood "Pre-Teen Kittens."

Religion is another central element of *Margaret*. Though Blume herself had grown up fully Jewish, she wrote Margaret as an interfaith character. Blume would later explain that choice as curiosity about her brother's marrying outside the religion.[2] In the book, Margaret tries to reconcile both her Christian and Jewish heritage, creating her own unique relationship with God in the process. "Though Judaism was a part of me, like having brown eyes, my relationship with God had almost nothing to do with organized religion. Like Margaret, God was my confidante, my friend," Blume has said.[3]

> **Blume still felt closely in touch with the curious, confused girl she once was.**

Upon finishing the book, Blume was satisfied but unsure if the book would be well received. While writing it, Blume had followed her instincts, disregarding much of what she'd learned in Lee Wyndham's class. "I'd decided I was just going to let go—no rules, no regulations," Blume has said. "[Wyndham] had a list of 'Thou Shalt Nots' for children's books, but I thought, 'No,' [because] I remembered what life was like in sixth grade."[4]

When *Margaret* was published in 1970, it became clear that Blume's gamble had paid off. Dorothy Broderick, a well-known librarian and literacy advocate, raved about the book in *The New York Times*, which later named *Margaret* "Outstanding Book of the Year." Blume was heartened by the positive feedback: "It wasn't until I read [Broderick's] review that I thought, 'My God! Maybe I can really do this!'"[5]

Yet not everyone was jumping on the Blume bandwagon. Though critics praised *Margaret* for its frank portrayal of a teen's view of sex and religion, the book raised eyebrows among conservative parents and educators. At Randy and Larry's elementary school, the principal forbade *Margaret* from the library shelves for its mentions of menstruation.[6] Though the content may seem tame by modern standards, it was unprecedented at the time of its release. Today, adults and kids alike view *Margaret* as a classic, spawning now-legendary anthems like, "I must, I must, I must increase my bust!"

In 1971, Blume tackled the topic of puberty once again. This time, she adopted a thirteen-year-old boy's point of view. In *Then Again, Maybe I Won't*, the book's main character, Tony Miglione, keeps many secrets inside, from his friend's shoplifting problem to his secret crushes to his nightly wet dreams. Looking back, Blume holds a special place for the book in her heart: "*Then Again* is one of those special 'kids' of mine. I loved being a boy for the eight months I was writing it."[7]

As Blume's personal library of "kids" grew, so did her own children. Randy was ten years old now and Larry was eight. Blume often thought back to their earliest years, which provided her with endless amusement. One particular memory had given her the inspiration for *Freckle Juice*, which was also published in 1971. When Randy had taken baths as a toddler, she had often mixed together baby powder, shampoo, and soap. Calling her special concoction "freckle juice," Randy would pat it all over her baby face.[8] Unable to pass up such a catchy title, Blume took the concept and spun it into a hit book. The plot featured a young boy who uses a "magical" potion to erase his freckle face.

Blume's child-raising experiences proved rich material for inspiration. For her next project, Blume would immortalize Larry's toddler antics. Many years before, she had written a picture book called *Peter, Fudge, and Dribble*. The story was based on an article her babysitter had found about a boy swallowing a pet turtle.[9] At the urging of literary editor Ann Durell, Blume adapted the work into a longer book called *Tales of a Fourth Grade Nothing*. Set in a New York City apartment building much like where Mary Sullivan's family lived, the book told the humorous tale of Peter Hatcher and his brother Fudge. (The Fudge character was based on young Larry.) Published in 1972, the book would later spawn a highly successful series of Fudge books.

In 1974, Blume's kids shone on the printed page yet again. *The Pain and the Great One* centered on a brother and sister, based on Larry and Randy at ages six and eight. A picture book for younger readers, the book takes a lighthearted look at sibling relationships. More than thirty years later, Blume now counts the project as her favorite book she's written for that age group.[10]

As Blume explored her special connection to her children, she questioned her bond with her husband, John. Throughout the years, numerous families in her suburban New Jersey neighborhood had split up. Blume suppressed her own unhappiness in hopes of avoiding the same outcome. "I wrote *It's Not the End of the World* at that time, to try to answer some of my children's questions about divorce, to let other kids know they were not alone and perhaps, because I was not happy in my marriage," Blume once said. "For years I would not, could not, admit that we had any problems. The perfect daughter had become the perfect wife and mother."[11]

In 1975, Blume could no longer ignore her crumbling relationship. After sixteen years of marriage, she and John decided to divorce. Blume broke the news to her children by writing each of them a heartfelt letter.[12] Like her kids, Blume was devastated; part of her felt like she did not know how to be alone.[13] She had married John while still in college, and that way of life was all Blume knew. It was not long before Blume struck up a romance with physicist Thomas Kitchens. Confiding in and spending time with Kitchens made her feel safe and secure once again.

Kitchens had just relocated to London for a temporary job, and Blume decided a change of scenery might be a fitting way to ease the family's pain. With Randy and Larry in tow, Blume moved overseas to be closer to Kitchens. In May 1976, Kitchens and Blume were married after a very short courtship. During the brief time they spent in England, Blume began to have serious doubts about her decision. "Before long, it became clear that this hasty new marriage wasn't going to work and I didn't know what to do about it or how to get out of it without looking like a fool, to John, to my children, to my mother, to the world."[14]

After the school semester in London was complete, Kitchens received another job offer in Los Alamos, New Mexico, and the family moved once again. Upon her arrival in New Mexico, Blume decided to rent an office rather than work from home. The office space was right above a bakery, and Blume could not resist the inviting smells drifting up to her typewriter. "Every day at noon, I would rush downstairs to buy two glazed donuts, and by three o'clock, I would crave another round. After a few months and a few pounds, I moved home again," remembers Blume on her Web site.[15]

Though Blume was questioning the marriage, she tried to keep up the "perfect" facade as in the past. "When I remarried so quickly, I wanted my kids to like, accept, respect, even love my new husband. . . . I would say, 'Isn't he wonderful?' And my kids would look at me as if I were crazy."[16] After three years of marriage, the couple ended the relationship. Soon after, Blume and the children found a house in Santa Fe. At this point, moving was status quo for the Blume family. Between 1972 and 1978, Randy and Larry had attended six different schools in New Jersey, England, and New Mexico.[17]

Though Blume was questioning the marriage, she tried to keep up the "perfect" facade.

Blume recalls those three years as some of the darkest of her life. She credits writing with helping her through the rough times. Divorce became a theme in several of her future books, including 1983's *Smart Women* (for adults) and 1987's *Just as Long as We're Together*. The breathtaking New Mexico locale also provided ample inspiration. Blume's Southwest surroundings became the setting for *Tiger Eyes*, one of her most poignant works. ("The scenery is so beautiful, I have to face the wall to work," Blume once told interviewer Betsy Lee.[18])

In the book, fifteen-year-old Davey's father is violently killed in a robbery, and the family moves to New Mexico to work through their grief. Though the idea was originally hatched as a screenplay, Blume disagreed with the producer's creative direction and adapted it into a book.[19] "It is a story about violence and the aftermath of violence, and they wanted the father to die of a heart attack spelunking in northern New Mexico. . . . They wanted to change everything about the story and I couldn't do that," Blume told interviewer Maryann Weidt.[20] Writing *Tiger Eyes* was an especially personal experience for Blume, who later realized the book's theme was rooted in her own sudden, painful loss of her father.[21]

In 1980, Blume finally met a man that would become "the one"—George Cooper, a professor of law at Columbia University. Initially, Blume was skeptical about giving love another chance, but optimism won out. They later married on the balcony of their New York City apartment in 1987.[22] Recalling those years and her *Tiger Eyes* film near-debacle, Blume told *The New York Times*: "My son says I meet someone and say, 'This is a nice person, why not work with this person?' I must say I'm also guilty of having married that way. I just lucked out with George. And for once, I waited—seven years—to marry him."[23]

Chapter 6

A Voice for Females, Fighting to Be Heard

When Blume began writing in the late sixties, she never expected that her work would become globally known and loved. She simply viewed writing as a way of expressing her creativity. Yet her straightforward approach to storytelling has earned her the respect and loyalty of countless fans. Ironically, the fact that Blume has always "told it like it is" has been a double-edged sword. Three of her most popular works have also been the targets of widespread book-banning campaigns and criticism: *Deenie*, *Blubber*, and *Forever*.

Published in 1973, *Deenie* told the story of Deenie Fenner, a girl whose dreams of being a model are dashed after learning that she has scoliosis. In the book, Deenie must cope with the difficulties of wearing a back brace and having an unsupportive mother. With her appearance drastically altered, Deenie must also rethink her own standard of beauty. Reads one excerpt:

> When we left Dr. Kliner's office, I was wearing the brace with Helen's skirt and shirt over it. I was kind of scared that Ma would start crying again when she saw me. Instead she said, "Well, that's not bad at all. You can hardly tell you're wearing it, Deenie." I knew from the catch in her voice that she was just saying it and didn't mean a single word. Daddy asked, "How does it feel?"
> "Like I'm in a cage," I said.[1]

Deenie had its roots in reality. Blume was inspired to write the book after meeting a fourteen-year-old girl with scoliosis in 1970. While working on the project, she spent a day at the hospital observing the way children were fitted for back braces.[2] As tribute to her realistic portrayal of the affliction, letters of praise poured in from hundreds of fans going through similar struggles.[3] Yet despite Blume's admirable work, many parents and librarians took issue with several references to masturbation and sexual desire. When the book was banned from some shelves and reading lists, the fan support poured in once again.

"When *Deenie* was banned, I got wonderful letters," Blume told National Public Radio in 2004. "One of my favorites was from two 13-year-olds who said, 'So we've read this book, and we can't find the reason that it was banned.'"[4] Despite the seemingly tame content, *Deenie* has emerged as Blume's most oft-challenged work over the years.[5]

In 1974, Blume tackled a new topic: cruelty in the classroom. While earlier books such as *Margaret* had explored the dynamics of female relationships, *Blubber* took the social scrutiny to new levels. The book's main character, Jill Brenner, is part of a popular group that relentlessly bullies shy, overweight Linda. When the tables are eventually turned on Jill, she learns what it is like to go from predator to prey. The book was based on an experience Blume's daughter Randy had in fifth grade. One of Randy's classmates was locked in a closet and put on trial for no apparent reason—other than being unliked.[6] The scene is recreated in *Blubber*:

> Robby and Irwin shoved Linda into the closet. Then they slammed the door and Wendy turned the key, leaving it in the lock. "Let me out of here," Linda called. Her voice was muffled. "Just shut up and listen to me, Blubber," Wendy said. "You're on trial for being a stool pigeon, a rat, a fink, and a tattle-tale. How do you plead . . . guilty or not guilty?"[7]

Like *Deenie*, *Blubber* came under fire for its brutal examination of bullying and use of adult language. Between 1982 and 1992, the book was removed from library shelves no less than thirteen times.[8] Eventually, it was named one of the American Library Association's "100 Most Frequently Challenged Books of 1990–1999."[9] In one Ohio elementary school, school officials balked because "bad is never punished. Good never comes to the fore. Evil is triumphant."[10] Yet

Blume felt that the book's refusal to end "happily ever after" was more reflective of real life. She also defended its use of profanity, saying: "The one thing I wanted desperately to do in *Blubber* . . . was to let [fifth graders] use the language they really use. . . . Children in America who ride school buses use all the four-letter words freely."[11]

> **Blume felt that [*Blubber*'s] refusal to end "happily ever after" was more reflective of real life.**

By the time *Forever* was published in 1975, Blume had established herself as a champion of realism. Her books provided a refreshing change of pace for young readers. Yet *Forever* was about to cement her status as a daring young author. The book's plot centered around Katherine and Michael, a high-school couple who decide to become sexually active. Its characters explored the emotional and physical highs and lows that accompany first love, as well as the inherent responsibilities. Blume had been urged to write the book by a teenage Randy, who had asked, "Couldn't there ever be a book about two nice, smart kids who do it, and nobody has to die?"[12]

The book was an instant classic among teenagers. They appreciated its ability to rise above locker-room talk without being preachy. One *Guardian Unlimited* writer later summed up its appeal by saying, "We'd giggled through sex education classes and blushed through awkward parental conversations, but none of us had ever come across anything like this: a book that discussed sex frankly, but placed it in the context of normal teenage life—school, friends, family, a loving relationship."[13]

Once again, conservatives did not take kindly to the content of *Forever*. They believed that the book did not "promote abstinence and monogamous relationships." Schools from Florida to Ohio to Pennsylvania objected to the book's use of profanity and what they deemed explicit conversations about sex.[14] At one Colorado school, an enterprising sixth grader petitioned the library to keep Judy Blume books in circulation. At another school where the book had been banned, students wore "Judy Blume for Principal" and "Judy Blume for President" buttons to school every day.[15]

Blume was perplexed and dismayed by the uprising. From the time her children were young, she had vowed to be incredibly open with them about sexuality—in stark contrast to her own upbringing.[16] She could not understand why other parents deprived their own children of the same information: "How are young people supposed to make thoughtful decisions if they don't have information and no one is willing to talk with them? Girls and boys have to learn to say 'no' or 'not without a condom' without fear."[17]

Despite the controversy, executives at CBS embraced the story. The network approached

Blume with an offer of a made-for-television movie. In 1978, *Forever* hit the airwaves, starring Stephanie Zimbalist as Katherine and Dean Butler as Michael. (Both actors went on to have successful film and television careers.) Set to music by Fleetwood Mac and other popular seventies artists, the movie did an impressive job of translating the tender tale to the screen. "I was totally pleased with it," Blume has said. "They had an executive producer who fought the network to be able to make it true to the book."[18]

On the heels of Blume's work hitting the small screen, 1978 brought another exciting milestone. Blume was asked to address the attendees of the American Booksellers Association in Atlanta, along with authors Dr. Seuss and Maurice Sendak.[19] It was an exciting accomplishment for Blume. She had come full circle from the days of channeling Dr. Seuss while doing the dishes!

Though her success had reached new heights, becoming the target of censorship was a difficult adjustment for Blume. She felt alienated and resentful that her work was not reaching its intended audience. While the seventies had been a time of relatively little backlash, the eighties ushered in the height of the book-banning craze. In her introduction to *Places I Never Meant to Be*, Blume muses about the change of mind-set:

> The seventies were a good decade for writers and readers . . . We were free to write about real kids in the real world. Kids with feelings and emotions, kids with real families, kids like we once were. And

young readers gobbled up our books, hungry for characters with whom they could identify. . . .

Then, almost overnight, following the presidential election of 1980, the censors crawled out of the woodwork. . . . Not only would they decide what their children could read but what all children could read. It was the beginning of the decade that wouldn't go away, that still won't go away almost twenty years later. Suddenly books were seen as dangerous to young minds.[20]

Feeling the effects of censorship, however, was nothing new to Blume. She had learned just how stifling it could be as a fifth-grader, when her mother forbade Blume from reading John O'Hara's *A Rage to Live* until she grew up. When O'Hara's name appeared on Blume's high-school reading list years later, she had raced to the library to check out the book. Yet Blume's excitement was quashed after learning that *A Rage to Live* was on the library's "restricted" list. The book could not be read without parental consent. She had not understood the mentality behind book banning then, and decades later, she still could not.

By the time Blume met up with the National Coalition Against Censorship director, Leanne Katz, Blume had reached a peak point of frustration. Her books were being continually called into question. Some had even been grouped with Salman Rushdie's highly controversial *Satanic Verses* in a 1989 library demonstration.[21] Yet once embraced by Katz's network of like-minded advocates for free speech, Blume felt reinvigorated by their fiery dedication. "Once I started to work with Leanne on the behalf of freedom to read and choose your own books, I become empowered. I felt that I wasn't alone anymore."[22]

In 1999, Blume took action by editing *Places I Never Meant to Be*. The anthology featured original stories by well-known censored writers. All royalties from the project benefited the National Coalition Against Censorship. The book was dedicated to Leanne Katz, who died of cancer in 1997. That same year, Blume wrote an editorial for *The New York Times* titled "Is Harry Potter Evil?" The opinion piece questioned decisions to remove the popular fantasy series from library shelves and classrooms.

In 2003, Blume continued to spearhead efforts in support of *Potter*. A family based in Cedarville, Arkansas, had filed a headline-making lawsuit against the local school board for restricting library access to the *Potter* series. The school board's reasoning was that the books sent dangerous messages about witchcraft and rebellion against authority. In response, Blume joined forces with numerous free-speech advocacy groups to file an amicus brief. (Amicus briefs are filed by parties who are not directly involved in a lawsuit, but have relevant information to the case.) The brief stated that the board's decision violated young readers' First Amendment rights. Their efforts did not go unrecognized. In April 2003, the books were restored to unrestricted library shelves.

"It's not just the books under fire now that worry me. It is the books that will never be written.

The books that will never be read. And all due to the fear of censorship. As always, young readers will be the real losers," reads a statement on Blume's Web site.[23]

Despite Blume's active stance against censorship, the book-banning climate persists. This reality has resulted in some interesting ethical conundrums, especially during the editing process. After Blume turned in the manuscript for *Tiger Eyes* in the early eighties, her editor, Richard Jackson, asked her to omit a scene in which the main character explores her sexuality after her father's violent death. Though Blume felt the scene was a turning point in the character's emotional journey, she agreed to make the change. "My editor agreed that [the scene] made sense psychologically, but he wanted the book to reach as many readers as possible," says Blume.

> "As always, young readers will be the real losers."
> —Judy Blume on censorship

"Because we were in the midst of a book banning craze, he knew that line would cause problems. So I took it out."[24]

Blume found herself torn once again many years later while working on *Here's to You, Rachel Robinson*. In the book, Rachel, a type-A overachiever, struggles to understand her older brother Charles's rebellious behavior. In one emotionally charged exchange, Charles angrily uses a curse word during a sarcastic toast to the Robinson family.

Though Blume was asked to take out the profanity, she felt that doing so would compromise her ability to stay true to the character. Blume told interviewer RoseEtta Stone: "[In deciding], I talked to my grown son who reminded me how important it is to write honestly. He said something like, 'You're Judy Blume. If you give in, there's no hope.' I cried over that one."[25] In the end, the line went unchanged, alienating some of Blume's fans but allowing Blume to maintain her integrity.

In 2004, the American Library Association named Blume the second-most censored author of the previous fifteen years.[26] Though her opponents have been extremely vocal, the devotion of her readers speaks even louder. In his article, "Why Judy Blume Endures," Yale professor Mark Oppenheimer speaks to this fact: "Teachers never assigned her books. But when I got to college, there was no author, except Shakespeare, whom more of my peers had read."[27]

Chapter 7

All in the Family

Millions of Judy Blume books have been printed over the years, leaving little doubt as to her enduring popularity. Though *Are You There, God? It's Me, Margaret* is the first book that most associate with Blume, the Fudge collection has arguably earned her more readers than any of her other books. Thanks to their endearing take on sibling rivalry and family life, both kids and adults can easily relate to the series—and the sales figures show it. Both *Tales for a Fourth Grade Nothing* and *Superfudge* hold court on *Publisher's Weekly*'s list of the "25 All-Time Bestselling Children's Books" in paperback.[1] The series has also been a critics' darling, having earned more than fifty book awards.

In a sense, Fudge has grown up with Blume's

children. Spanning the decades of Blume's career, four books form Fudge's legacy: *Tales of a Fourth Grade Nothing* (1972), *Superfudge* (1980), *Fudge-a-Mania* (1990), and *Double Fudge* (2002). The series follows the antics, arguments, and affectionate moments of the Hatcher family.

In the first installment, fourth-grader Peter gets fed up with young Fudge's outrageous behavior and makes his own bid for his parents' attention. Many of the concepts in *Tales* were taken from picture books Blume wrote in her early career stages. One such book, *Mrs. Crater's Worries*, told the tale of a child who refused to eat. It was later adapted into Chapter 3 of *Tales*, "The Family Dog," in which Fudge's hunger strike drives the family crazy.[2] The character of Sheila Tubman (from *Otherwise Known . . .*) is also introduced in this book as Peter's nemesis and neighbor. Readers could not get enough of the book, eventually gobbling up more than seven million copies.[3]

> **In a sense, Fudge has grown up with Blume's children.**

The demand for *Tales* made it clear to Blume that readers were hungry for more. She had received many letters from fans asking for a new *Fudge* book, but Blume wanted to wait until she got the perfect idea. In 1979, she got just that. "I remember exactly where I was when the idea finally came to me—in the shower, covered with soap and shampoo," she writes on her Web site. "And the idea seemed so simple I couldn't believe it had taken seven years. I would give the Hatchers a new baby."[4]

In *Superfudge*, the Hatchers relocate to Princeton, New Jersey, and await the arrival of baby daughter Tootsie. True to form, both Peter and Fudge have funny, relatable ways of dealing with these major changes. The book was a major hit right off the bat, selling 1.5 million copies in just six months.[5] Despite its family-friendly content, however, Blume once again found herself under the watchful censor's eye. Some readers objected to Fudge's confession that he does not really believe in Santa Claus. In the South, numerous schools refused to allow musical theater company Theatreworks to perform their production of *Superfudge* unless the scene was cut. Said Blume of the incident: "I probably could have stopped them, but I didn't. There are times when I'm just too weary to fight. You have to choose your battles."[6]

Another ten years would pass before the third installment, *Fudge-a-Mania*, was published. The premise for the book was born the summer of 1989, when Blume and her husband Cooper vacationed in Southwest Harbor, Maine. A tire swing in their summer home's backyard caused Blume to picture Sheila Tubman swinging away. Suddenly, she knew she wanted the Tubmans and the Hatchers to spend a summer in Maine together. (Cooper suggested "Fudge-a-Maine-ia" as the original title.) Says Blume, "This would be a reunion book. I'd bring the major characters from all the *Fudge* books together and that would be it—I'd never write about them again!"[7]

Blume's vow to say good-bye to the *Fudge* series was not to be kept. Her grandson, Elliott, was constantly begging Blume to write another. Her response was always the same: "If I get another idea, I promise I'll write one. But don't be disappointed because I doubt an idea will come to me."[8] Not surprisingly, Elliott ended up serving as the inspiration for the series' finale, *Double Fudge*. While eating at a Key West restaurant, Elliott asked Blume to buy him wearable art from a street vendor. When she replied that she had no cash, he directed her to the nearest cash machine![9] Hence Fudge's foray into fortune—*Double Fudge* centered on Fudge's newfound obsession with money and what it could buy.

In many ways, the *Fudge* series stands apart from Blume's other works. While writing the books, she strayed from her normal writing approach. Blume instead employed a quick, spontaneous writing style that she believed lent well to humor. "Unlike a novel, which can take me three years and up to twenty drafts, *Fudge* books either come or they don't. Maybe that's why I write so few of them," says Blume on her Web site. In fact, *Tales* is the only book Blume has ever written that was published "as-is" from the very first draft.[10]

Fudge found further fame as a Saturday morning television series. The show ran on ABC and CBS from 1995 to 1997. At first, Blume was thrilled when she was asked to live in Los Angeles temporarily as a consultant for the show. Yet her excitement turned to disappointment when she realized her input was not welcome. "It was terrible. I was referred to as *the writer of the original material*," she remembers.[11] Her reaction to the end result was somewhat ambivalent, with Blume deeming it "DNE: Does Not Embarrass."[12]

Family themes have also taken the forefront in Blume's nonfiction efforts. Because of her willingness to explore sensitive topics like divorce, growing up, and bullying, Blume received thousands of letters from fans going through real-life situations mirroring those in her books. After getting to know characters like Deenie and Margaret, readers felt they knew them intimately. It was easy to confide in Blume after her characters had shared their secrets with the world. In 1983, Blume began gathering letters for a project that later became *Letters to Judy: What Your Kids Wish They Could Tell You*.

With *Letters*, Blume hoped to bridge the gap between parents and children. In answering letters from kids grappling with everything from addiction to adoption, Blume shared her experiences along with her own special brand of support. "Like every parent, I made a million mistakes raising my kids, as you'll see when you read this book," she writes in the foreword. "And I certainly don't have all the answers. It's just a lot easier to sound wise when you're talking about someone else's family."[13]

Blume's other objective with *Letters* was to let her fans know that their letters were read with care. With more than two thousand letters coming in monthly, Blume was unable to respond to many of them. She answered as many as she could, and her hope was that the book would fill the gaps. "Only recently have I discovered why I'm not nearly as productive in my fiction writing as I used to be. It's because I spent at least half my workday answering letters," Blume once said.[14]

Proceeds from the book benefited the KIDS Fund, a nonprofit foundation Blume founded in 1981. The KIDS Fund was Blume's way of "giving back to the kids a little bit of what they've given to me."[15] With the fund, Blume provided grants of up to five thousand dollars for programs such as Kids in the Middle (a counseling program for children of divorce) and the Baltimore Council on Adolescent Pregnancy and Parenting Prevention. She had initially raised the seed money for the foundation with the proceeds from another nonfiction project, *The Judy Blume Diary: The Place to Put Your Own Feeling*. The *Diary* was intended to give kids a private place to express their thoughts and plan their futures.

An old saying goes, "Friends are the family you choose." Along with her focus on family, Blume enjoyed writing about the twists and turns of friendship, and the central plot of numerous books reflected that. Two such books comprise her only other series: *Just as Long as We're Together* and *Here's to You, Rachel Robinson*. Each book tells the story of a trio of seventh graders from a different perspective.

When Blume started writing *Just as Long as We're Together* in 1986, she was bursting with excitement. The characters had been incubating in her head for years, and she was itching to put them down on paper. While working on the book, Blume stored eighty pages of an early draft in her freezer. "What are you going to do if the freezer defrosts and all the ink runs?" a friend asked incredulously. Blume laughed about it, saying she had gone "truly crazy."[16]

> "I spent at least half my workday answering letters."
>
> —Judy Blume

As always, Blume looked to her real life for inspiration. She and George had been spending time in Westport, Connecticut, so several characters were named after Westport landmarks. (Main character Alison Monceau was named for furniture store Parc Monceau, and the Klaff twins were born of Klaff's plumbing supply store.[17]) For the title, Blume and her agent sang old campside songs, choosing a line from an old favorite called "Side by Side."

The final product, *Just as Long as We're Together*, was published in 1987. The book met with great fanfare by Blume's devotees. They had waited six years since Blume's last young adult book and could not wait to get their hands on a new story. Booksellers were also overjoyed. At the 1987 Booksellers Association meeting, some attendees took the galleys up to their hotel rooms and finished them in one sitting![18] The book focuses on two lifelong best friends, Stephanie and Rachel, who experience growing pains when a third friend, Alison, joins the fold. Narrated by Stephanie, the book also touches on divorce, first crushes, adoption, and weight struggles.

In 1993, the sequel, *Here's to You, Rachel Robinson*, was released. (Blume had originally hatched the idea as a trilogy, but the third book about Alison never came to light.[19]) The book continued the story of the three girls as told from overachieving Rachel's point of view. Blume based the character of Rachel on a perfectionist friend she had known in junior high and a twelve-year-old fan who had written about feeling alienated because she was already taking college courses.[20]

To Blume, it was important that readers not view the series as "message" books. "In *Just As Long As We're Together*, it's a story about three friends, really. I don't understand, you know, when someone says, 'This is a book about divorce,' because, of course, this book isn't. It's about people, as all fiction is, and what's happening in their lives at the time that you're telling their story."[21]

Chapter 8

Endless Summers

Philosopher Albert Camus once said, "In the depth of winter, I finally learned that within me there lay an invincible summer." The same might be said of Blume. Though she had experienced plenty of dark times in her life, she had always emerged with renewed strength and broader perspective. Perhaps because of its carefree, hopeful nature, the season of summer has always been meaningful to Blume. "Summer is my season, the season I wait for the rest of the year. You can live a lifetime in the summer, especially when you're young," says Blume on her Web site.[1]

Finding true love has also brightened Blume's life considerably. At the 2004 National Book Awards ceremony, she said, "I sometimes accuse [my husband George] of having wrecked my career because in our 25 years together I've been happy, and contentment isn't nearly as good for writing as angst."[2] Summer has played a major role in their relationship, serving as the backdrop for many memorable trips and turning points.

Serendipity played a role in introducing Cooper and Blume. They had met while Blume and her children were living in New Mexico in the early eighties. Cooper's twelve-year-old daughter, Amanda, also resided there at the time. During one of Cooper's visits from New York, he was given a list of possible dinner dates. When Cooper showed the list to Amanda, she immediately recognized Blume's name and screamed at the prospect of her dad dating her favorite author. "He denies that he says this now, but he used to tell me that his response was: 'Not that woman who writes those books that you read over and over and over again!'" Blume told *The Washington Post*.[3]

> ## "Contentment isn't nearly as good for writing as angst."
> —Judy Blume

Once the couple began dating, it became clear that both viewed life as an unfolding adventure. While Blume had felt forced to fit into a certain mold in previous relationships, she felt a sense of freedom with Cooper. An avid sailor, Cooper convinced Blume to take sailing lessons with him.

"When George and I met . . . he said I'd make the ideal mate if only I knew how to sail," Blume has said laughingly. "So I went to sailing camp, where I was an absolute, total failure. Three hours a day studying the physics of sailing, and the only way I know which way the wind is blowing is by which way my hair sticks out."[4] Though Blume did not take to the water quite as Cooper had hoped, there was no doubt that the two had taken to each other for life.

Yet life as a stepfamily was not always smooth sailing for Blume, Cooper, and their kids. When Blume gushed to Randy about her new relationship, Randy replied wearily, "Don't tell me who to like, Mother. I'll make up my own mind."[5] Cooper's daughter also experienced some resentment at the beginning. Says Blume in *Letters to Judy*, "[Amanda] thought, 'Wow . . . Judy Blume . . . wait till I tell my friends who my father is living with!' I think she was disappointed when she found out that I am just an ordinary person and that life with me wouldn't be perfect."[6]

Over time, a comfortable dynamic between the merging families settled in, and Blume and Cooper decided to tie the knot. Fittingly, the couple chose to be married during the summertime—June 6, 1987, to be exact. In an informal ceremony on the couple's balcony overlooking Central Park, the two said, "I do." Then the couple was off for a honeymoon in New Hampshire, where Blume also made time to fit in a speaking engagement for eight hundred children.[7]

Blume and Cooper discovered their shared love of summer in 1983, when they decided to leave Santa Fe for a summer on Martha's Vineyard. Though Blume had grown up on the East Coast, she had never visited the popular vacation spot. She was intrigued by this inviting and mysterious new place. The couple made plans to rent a summer home without viewing it first. What awaited them was a "rundown place hidden in the woods, surrounded by tall pine trees. Unless you looked out the windows of the second floor, you might not have known it was on the water. My stepdaughter, Amanda, who was fifteen that summer, named it 'Psycho House.'"[8] (The "Psycho House" reference would later make its way into *Summer Sisters*.)

Psycho House was set on a pond, and each afternoon Blume set out in the dinghy for some alone time. One day, Blume was rowing along when the idea for *Summer Sisters* came to her suddenly. Though she would not begin work on the book for another ten years, the concept had taken vivid shape. "It was just a vague idea then—two young women from very different families in Santa Fe spend a series of summers on the Vineyard, one the guest of the other's family," Blume says on her Web site.[9] In the following summers that she and Cooper returned to the Vineyard, the smells, sights, and experiences provided additional detail for *Summer Sisters*.

Even the less idyllic summers provided ample inspiration for Blume. In 1989, she and Cooper summered in Southwest Harbor, Maine. There she

Judy Blume arrives for the Quill Awards Gala at the Museum of Natural History in New York City on October 10, 2006.

got the idea for *Fudge-a-Mania*. All the right factors were in place to reunite the Hatchers and Tubmans for a summer adventure. Blume had just completed work on a television movie based on *Otherwise Known as Sheila the Great* and was looking to resurrect the characters. "It was a cold, damp summer, a disappointment to us, but as it turned out, a great summer for writing. I set the book in Southwest Harbor and had fun using the names of local shops and characters," writes Blume on her Web site.[10]

Today, Blume and Cooper own several residences. The couple divides their time between New York City, Key West, and Martha's Vineyard. Their house on the Vineyard lies on the same pond as Psycho House, with a breathtaking view of the sea. On the outskirts of the house lie three cabins, one of which acts as Blume's creative haven. Dubbed "Cuckoo" by the previous owner, Blume's writing cabin is "not much bigger than a doll's house." She does her work from a picnic table that doubles as a desk.[11]

Cuckoo served as the locale for Blume's almost torturous working experience on *Summer Sisters*, a poignant, daring story of two friends coming of age. Blume was extremely hard on herself, completing almost twenty drafts over five years. Typically, Blume's writing process is somewhat less time-consuming.

She begins by keeping a notebook for several months of ideas, dialogue snippets, character sketches, and imaginative doodles. Often, Blume's ideas have spent years developing in her head, so the notebook scrawlings flow freely. Once she begins work, the notebook acts as her "security blanket."[12]

Blume's first drafts, which she dubs her "thinking drafts," are the most dreaded part of the process for Blume.[13] To get through it, she prefers to work rapidly without self-editing. Says Blume, "I find that when I'm doing a first draft, it's important for me to keep going. Otherwise, I get into revising each scene a million times and never move ahead."[14]

> Often, Blume's ideas have spent years developing in her head.

Almost immediately after finishing the first draft, Blume dives into the second. The rewriting process is something that Blume relishes. "During the next two rewrites, I work longer hours and with more enthusiasm. By the third draft, I'm so into the characters, I have to be dragged away from my desk," she told fellow children's author Cynthia Leitich Smith.[15] After the third draft is perfected, Blume finally feels ready to send it to her editor for the first time. Together they discuss the manuscript's strengths and weaknesses, after which Blume completes another revision.

Blume's writing habits are just as disciplined as her unique process. In the morning, Blume gets dressed and pretends as if she were going to an office. After eating breakfast, she then holes up in her work space until lunchtime. Blume works efficiently in order to free the rest of her day for family and relaxation. "Since I'm a daytime-only writer, I've never had trouble finding time for a personal life. . . . It's important for me to get out and be with people," Blume has said. "I go to the movies. I work out at the gym. I kayak. I ride my bike. I take long walks, and often get my best ideas when I'm not at the computer."[16]

Being outdoors provides much inspiration for Blume. Whether biking in Key West or kayaking in Martha's Vineyard, Blume is constantly taking in her surroundings. ("Specifically, I can run down my books and tell you exactly where the ideas came from visually," Blume once told interviewer Justin Wintle.[17]) The couple's home in Key West is an "indoor-outdoor house" that keeps her connected to nature. "My [writing] desk faces a lush tropical garden. When I slide the doors open, I feel as if I'm working outdoors," Blume writes on her Web site. "I can't imagine a better place to write."[18] In Blume's eternal summertime, the living is definitely fine.

Chapter 9

With Risk Comes Reward

Four decades after Blume began writing, her career is set to come full circle. One of Blume's early books, *The Pain and the Great One*, is gaining new life. The book has always held sentimental value for Blume because the characters were based on Larry and Randy (who, as adults, still refer to each other by those nicknames).[1] Currently, Blume is at work on a new illustrated series featuring the same siblings. The first of the four books, *The Pain and the Great One: Soupy Saturdays*, was released in August 2007.

Like *The Pain and the Great One*, many of Blume's other books have demonstrated a timeless appeal. Yet their longevity has made it necessary that certain details evolve with the times. New editions of *Forever* include a foreword that warns readers about the dangers of HIV and using birth-control pills without additional protection.[2] In the late nineties, Margaret's belted sanitary napkins were replaced with more modern products like tampons and winged pads.

Though some readers were incensed by the *Margaret* decision, Blume stands by the changes. "I'm not taking out her velvet party dress. I'm not taking out her giant hair rollers, but just the *equipment*," Blume told the *Boston Phoenix* in 1998. "Some people said, 'Oh, no, it's a classic. You can't mess around with a classic.' And I said, 'Look, we're not messing around with the character or anything else. We're just messing around with the equipment.'"[3]

However, the "old-fashioned" aspects remain in many of Blume's books. In *It's Not the End of the World*, Karen's parents must go to Nevada if they want to go through with their divorce. In *Deenie*, many of the scoliosis treatments are now outdated. Even the way characters speak in some books shows signs of past times. In *Iggie's House*, one character proclaims she cannot play with "colored kids." Yet the believable characters and relatable plots of these books stand the test of time.

In a 1998 interview with National Public Radio, Ray Suarez asked Blume whether she worries about staying current with contemporary kids' slang. " Blume replied, "I'm not sure really that that's what gives dialogue the ring of truth.

I've never been big on trendy language. You know, what's trendy in California today is trendy in New York three months from now, and trendy somewhere else three years from now. I don't think that's what it's really all about. . . . Feelings [are] what it's all about."[4]

Indeed, Blume's special focus on kids' feelings has been the secret to her success. When reading about Margaret's bra-stuffing or Deenie's resentment about being "different," kids realize that they are not alone in their insecurities. This honest portrayal of adolescence has established Blume as one of the world's foremost young adult authors, having sold

> "Feelings [are] what it's all about."
>
> —Judy Blume

more than 75 million books. People of all ages light up upon hearing her name, remembering their own childhood experiences reading her books under the covers. "In certain important ways, she raised us all," wrote *Boston Phoenix* writer Ellen Barry.[5]

Blume often cringes when asked to choose her favorite book from her body of work. She compares the question to being asked to pick her favorite child; each holds special meaning. After all, story lines drawn from her own trials and travels are forever captured in their pages. When pressed for a reply, Blume says, "I suppose if I were forced to choose, I'd say *Fudge* because he's brought me so many readers; *Margaret* because she was my first character that kids identified with; and *Sally Freedman* because she's the character who's most like me."[6]

Although decades of censorship have made for a rocky road at times, Blume has emerged a strong champion of free speech. The self-admitted "people pleaser" from earlier years has become quite the opposite. Five of her books remain on the American Library Association's "100 Most Frequently Challenged" list,[7] and Blume has refused to back down in the face of controversy. "I don't set out to provoke—reviewers or librarians or anybody else," she once said. "I just think kids have certain rights, and they've been denied those rights for a long time."[8]

This willingness to take risks has earned due recognition from the publishing industry, especially in recent years. Her books have received close to one hundred awards in total, and Blume is held in high regard among her peers. In 2007, well-known female authors like Meg Cabot, Julie Kenner, and Stephanie Lessing banded together for an essay collection titled *Everything I Needed to Know About Being a Girl I Learned From Judy Blume*. Cabot wrote about how *Blubber* helped her survive being bullied, while Lessing confessed that *It's Not the End of the World* showed her that her *own* parents' divorce was not the end of the world.

In 1996, Blume received the Margaret A. Edwards Award for Lifetime Achievement from the American Library Association. Specifically honoring the book *Forever*, the award hailed Blume for "helping adolescents become aware of themselves and addressing questions about their role and importance in relationships, society, and in the world."[9] Other authors who have received this award in past years include S. E. Hinton (*The Outsiders*), Lois Lowry (*The Giver*), and Robert Cormier (*I Am the Cheese*).

Another major honor came Blume's way in 2004. The National Book Foundation chose Blume to receive the Medal for Distinguished Contribution to American Letters. The award put her in the company of past recipients like Ray Bradbury, Stephen King, and Oprah Winfrey. The first young adult author to receive the distinction, Blume was overwhelmed and overjoyed. In her acceptance speech, she gushed, "I can't believe I'm standing here, as my family will tell you. This honor was so totally unexpected it left me speechless and for months I remained speechless, even knowing I would have to stand up here tonight and deliver a 15 to 20 minute speech."[10]

Blume has received less refined tributes, such as the off-color comedy show *What Every Girl Should Know: An Ode to Judy Blume*. Playing to sold-out crowds at Chicago's Annoyance Theater in the late nineties, a group of improv comics poked fun at books like *Deenie* and *Forever*. Director Susan Messing described the show as "a combo platter of puberty, crooked spines and first love."[11]

Along with career highs, Blume has experienced

Shortly after receiving the Medal for Distinguished Contribution to American Letters, Judy Blume poses happily with husband George Cooper at the National Book Awards Ceremony and Dinner on November 17, 2004.

positive developments in her personal life. Cooper and Blume celebrated their twentieth wedding anniversary in 2007. The two continue to approach life with a *carpe diem* (seize the day) outlook. Splitting their time between several cities, the couple spends much of their time in mellow Key West. "My son says that all I need to do now is sit back and collect awards," Blume told *The Washington Post* in 2004. "I was, like, noooo! That's not what I want my future to be."[12]

Instead of resting on her laurels, Blume leads a very active life with Cooper in both their professional and residential communities. Besides continuing to write, Blume acts as a board member for the National Coalition Against Censorship, the Key West Literary Seminar, the Society of Children's Book Writers and Illustrators, and the Authors Guild. A film fanatic, Cooper founded the Key West Film Society in 1998. One of the society's labors of love has been the creation of the Tropic Cinema. A nonprofit movie theater, the Tropic showcases award-winning and independent films. Lectures, parties, and events are also regular occurrences. Says Blume, "George is still working 24/7, making sure everything runs smoothly. But he says he's never been happier."

When Cooper is not writing nonfiction or running the Tropic, he moonlights as Blume's webmaster. Together he and Blume have created an extensive Web site featuring biographical information, messages to her fans, writing tips, and little-known facts about her books. One look at the site's guest book acts as an instant testament to Blume's wide popularity. In just one day, readers from the United Arab Emirates to England to Canada logged on to wish Blume well.

Blume's children have also chosen creative professions. Randy, a licensed pilot, became a published author with *Crazy in the Cockpit* in 1999. Dedicated to Judy Blume, the book took a humorous look at what it is like to be a female pilot in a male-driven industry. A film director, Larry owns Tashmoo Productions in New York. In 2002, Blume produced and directed the independent film *Martin and Orloff*. Featuring many well-known comics, the madcap parody was well received by critics and viewers. In 2004, Tashmoo made a high-profile deal with Disney to bring *Deenie* to the big screen, but the project is currently on hold.[13]

Randy's son, Elliott, has an especially close relationship with Blume. Fittingly enough, his first word was "book" as a baby.[14] In his younger years, he loved to play "the *Fudge* game." Blume played four-year-old Fudge, while Elliott got to play big brother Peter. Often, they would playact different scenarios of the Hatchers, such as Coconut Fudge where Fudge is let loose on Key West.[15] Though Elliott is now in high school and has outgrown the *Fudge* game, he and Blume still indulge in other games such as ping-pong.[16]

Not surprisingly, Blume's books are just as relevant to his generation as they were thirty years ago. Though some of the references are outdated,

Judy Blume talks about her life and accomplishments at *Glamour*'s "Women of the Year" celebration in 2004.

the real-life scenarios ring just as true. Says professor Mark Oppenheimer, "In 1975, when the heroine of *Forever* decided to go on the pill, the book was daring. Now it is quaint. But it is precisely that quaintness that allows us to recognize Judy Blume properly. In this age of *Heather Has Two Mommies*, we clearly live after the flood. We might pause to thank the author who opened the gates."[17]

Reflecting back on her career, Blume often marvels at the direction it has taken. She had turned out books at a lightning pace in the seventies (at least one per year), taken on passion projects like *Letters to Judy* in the eighties, and had a runaway best seller in the nineties with *Summer Sisters*. She had never expected to become a household name, nor an author whose books would have an undeniable impact on millions of readers. Says Blume, "I do sometimes have to stop and say, 'I can't believe any of this is real.' My earliest prayers and fantasies were that someone would publish what I wrote. Then I got greedier and said, maybe someone will even *read* it. This is just beyond what I ever dreamed was possible."[18]

In Her Own Words

The following quotes from Judy Blume were derived from a variety of print and Web sources, including Blume's own *Letters to Judy*.

On her childhood:

"When I was very young, it was my father who made life seem exciting. Whether I was sitting on his workbench, hammering nails into a piece of wood, or painting the outside of my playhouse beside him, I felt safe and secure."[1]

"Recently, a friend asked, 'If you could go back and relive one year of your childhood, without being able to make any changes, which year would it be?' Without hesitation, I answered, 'Fourth grade in Miami Beach,' because in Miami Beach I learned to make new friends, I discovered an easygoing lifestyle that I had never known before, and I found out that moving isn't always so bad."[2]

"As a child, I knew that grown-ups kept secrets from me. I hated those secrets. I had a million questions about life but no one would tell me the answers. And most of all, from the age of nine, I wanted information on sexuality."[3]

On her special bond with her readers:

"I have a wonderful, intimate bond with kids. They feel that they know me and that I know them. I have this gift, this memory, so it's easy to project myself back to certain stages in my life. And I write about what I know is true of kids going through those same stages."[4]

"[My readers] write to me and say, 'You don't know me but you wrote this book about me, and I am Margaret.' If you ask me what do I do besides entertaining and making reading fun, it's creating characters with whom the kids can identify."[5]

"I feel very strongly that some of my books are private books, like *Margaret*, *Then Again, Maybe I Won't*, and *Deenie*—books that I see as a little visit between me and the child reader."[6]

On writing:

"My brother tells me that every book I write saves me five years in therapy."[7]

"On the best days, it's as if you are lost in another world. You don't know where the words are coming from. It's as if there's another part of your brain, a secret part, that just takes over."[8]

"[Every time I begin a new book] I ask myself, 'How am I going to fill up two hundred or three hundred pages?' But if I think of it as a whole book too soon, I'm going to scare myself. So I try to focus on one scene at a time. It may be just a page, it may be five or ten pages."[9]

"Through my worst years, my least stable years (following my divorce), I was still able to write. I can't explain how, but *Starring Sally J. Freedman as Herself*, *Wifey*, *Superfudge*, and the idea for *Tiger Eyes* came out of those four years. My angst was good for my work. I sometimes joke that finding happiness in my personal life has screwed up my career."[10]

"Oh, yes [I celebrate upon finishing a project]! But there's also a tremendous letdown. It's as if you have to say good-bye to your best friends, the people you've been so close to for a year or two or three."[11]

On censorship:

"It takes only one parent to challenge a book. It often takes a community to defend it."[12]

"[Book banning] is not just about sex anymore. It's not just about 'cuss' words. It's not just about witchcraft and Satanism. We've got the 'PC' crowd trying to ban *Huckleberry Finn*, and the 'sensitivity' teams combing through books looking for anything that might offend, anything that might make any child, any group uncomfortable. If they had their way, there wouldn't be much left in the library."[13]

"I think [the tendency to censor] comes from

adults who are fearful. It shows a lack of respect for young readers. It's almost as if children like it, there must be something wrong with it."[14]

"My husband and I like to reminisce about how, when we were nine, we read straight through L. Frank Baum's *Oz* series, books filled with wizards and witches. And you know what those subversive tales taught us? That we loved to read!"[15]

Chronology

1938—Born February 12 in Elizabeth, New Jersey.

1946—Family relocates temporarily to Miami Beach, Florida.

1956—Graduates with high honors from Battin High School.

1959—Randolph Sussman dies; Judy and John Blume marry.

1961—Obtains degree from New York University; daughter Randy is born.

1963—Son Larry is born.

1969—Publishing debut with *The One in the Middle is the Green Kangaroo*.

1970—*Are You There, God? It's Me, Margaret* receives "Outstanding Book of the Year" award from the *New York Times*.

1975—*Forever* creates a controversial stir among censors.

1978—Writes first book for adults, *Wifey*.

1980—*Superfudge* is released; Meets George Cooper.

1987—Esther Sussman passes away; Blume receives an honorary doctorate degree from Kean College in New Jersey.

1988—*The Judy Blume Memory Book* is printed, with proceeds going to the KIDS Fund.

1991—*Otherwise Known as Sheila the Great* is adapted into a made-for-television movie by Blume and her son.

1996—Selected by the American Library Association for a lifetime achievement award.

1998—Embarks on a major publicity tour for
bestseller *Summer Sisters*.
2003—Delivers commencement address at Mount
Holyoke College.
2004—Named *Glamour*'s Woman of the Year.
2007—Returns to her picture-book roots with *Soupy
Saturdays*.

Selected Works of Judy Blume

1969   *The One in the Middle Is the Green Kangaroo*

1970   *Iggie's House*

       Are You There, God? It's Me, Margaret

1971   *Freckle Juice*

       Then Again, Maybe I Won't

1972   *It's Not the End of the World*

       Otherwise Known as Sheila the Great

       Tales of a Fourth Grade Nothing

1973   *Deenie*

1974   *Blubber*

       The Pain and the Great One

1975   *Forever*

1977   *Starring Sally J. Freedman as Herself*

1978   *Wifey*

1980   *Superfudge*

1981   *Tiger Eyes*

1983	*Smart Women*
1986	*Letters to Judy: What Your Kids Wish They Could Tell You*
1987	*Just as Long as We're Together*
1990	*Fudge-a-Mania*
1993	*Here's to You, Rachel Robinson*
1998	*Summer Sisters*
1999	*Places I Never Meant to Be: Original Stories by Censored Writers*
2002	*Double Fudge*
2007	*The Pain and the Great One: Soupy Saturdays*

Chapter Notes

Chapter 1. Anything But Ordinary

1. Judy Blume, "Welcome to My Website," *JudyBlume.com*, n.d., <http://judyblume.com/message.html> (April 29, 2007).

2. Ibid.

3. Judy Blume, "Best Friends," *JudyBlume.com*, n.d., <http://www.judyblume.com/scrapbook.html> (April 29, 2007).

4. Judy Blume, *Summer Sisters* (New York: Dell Publishing, 1998), p. 29.

5. Judy Blume, "Best Friends," *JudyBlume.com*.

6. "Author Chat with Judy Blume," *Teenlink.nypl.org*, November 19, 2002, <http://teenlink.nypl.org/blume_txt.html> (April 29, 2007).

7. Judy Blume, "Judy Blume Talks About Writing," *JudyBlume.com*, n.d., <http://www.judyblume.com/writing-jb.html> (April 29, 2007).

8. Jennifer Frey, "Fiction Heroine," *The Washington Post*, November 17, 2004, <http://www.washingtonpost.com/wp-dyn/articles/A55767-2004Nov16.html> (April 29, 2007).

9. Judy Blume, "Judy's Anxiety Diary," *JudyBlume.com*, May 3, 1998, <http://www.judyblume.com/ss-diary1.html> (April 29, 2007).

10. Margot E. Edelman, "Tome Raider: Summer Sisters," *The Harvard Crimson*, March 1, 2006, <http://www.thecrimson.com/article.aspx?ref= 511702> (April 29, 2007).

11. Cynthia Leitich Smith, "Interview with Judy Blume," *CynthiaLeitichSmith.com*, 2002, <http://www.cynthialeitichsmith.com/lit_ resources/authors/interviews/JudyBlume.html> (April 29, 2007).

12. "All-Time Bestselling Children's Books," *PublishersWeekly.com*, December 17, 2001, <http://www.publishersweekly.com/index.asp? layout=article&articleid=CA187127> (April 29, 2007).

Chapter 2. Wartime Stories

1. "History," *City of Elizabeth*, 2006, <http:// www.elizabethnj.org/history.html> (June 21, 2007).

2. Judy Blume, "National Book Awards 2004 Acceptance Speech," *NationalBook.org*, November 17, 2004, <http://www.nationalbook. org/nbaacceptspeech_jblume04.html> (April 29, 2007).

3. Tracy Chevalier, *Twentieth Century Children Writers* (New York: St. James Press, 1989).

4. Leonard Marcus, *Author Talk: Conversations with Judy Blume, et al.* (New York: Simon & Schuster, 2000), p. 5.

5. "Autobiographical Statement," *Eighth Book of Junior Authors and Illustrators*, 2000, <http:// www.edupaperback.org/showauth2.cfm?authid= 15> (April 29, 2007).

6. Betsy Lee, *Judy Blume's Story* (Minneapolis, Minn.: Dillon Press, 1981), p. 13.

7. Ibid.

8. Marcus, p. 4.

9. Lee, p. 14.

10. Judy Blume, *Starring Sally J. Freedman as Herself* (New York: Yearling Books, 1978), p. 7.

11. Judy Blume, "Judy Blume's Books: Starring Sally J. Freedman as Herself," *JudyBlume.com*, n.d., <http://www.judyblume.com/sally.html> (April 29, 2007).

12. Marcus, p. 4.

13. "Autobiographical Statement."

14. Judy Freeman, "Talking with Judy Blume," *Instructor*, May/June 2005, <http://www.findarticles.com/p/articles/mi_mOSTR/is_8_114/ai_n13776899> (April 29, 2007).

15. Judy Blume, *Letters to Judy* (New York: G.P. Putnam's Sons, 1986), p. 132.

16. "Autobiographical Statement."

17. Blume, *Letters to Judy*, p. 61.

18. Maryann Weidt, *Presenting Judy Blume* (New York: Dell Publishing, 1990), p. 21.

19. "Autobiographical Statement."

20. Ibid.

21. Dick Gordon, "National Public Radio: The Connection," *TheConnection.org*, September 22, 2004, <http://www.theconnection.org/shows/2004/09/20040922_b_main.asp> (April 29, 2007).

22. Marcus, p. 5.

23. Lee, p. 21.

24. "Judy Blume's Interview Transcript," *Scholastic.com*, n.d., <http://content.scholastic.com/browse/collateral.jsp?id=10560_type=Contributor_typeId=1310> (April 29, 2007).

25. Judy Blume, "National Book Awards 2004 Acceptance Speech," *NationalBook.org*.

Chapter 3. Little Dreams, Big Talent

1. "All Things Considered," *National Public Radio*, September 15, 2004, <http://www.npr.org/templates/story/story.php?storyId=3919695> (April 29, 2007).

2. Cee Telford, *Judy Blume* (New York: Rosen Publishing Group: 2004), p. 13.

3. Elisa Ludwig, *Who Wrote That? Judy Blume* (Langhorne, Pa.: Chelsea House Publishers, 2004), p. 23.

4. "Spotlight On . . . Judy Blume," *RandomHouse.com*, 2004, <http://www.randomhouse.com/teachers/authors/results.pperl?authorid=2611> (April 29, 2007).

5. Betsy Lee, *Judy Blume's Story* (Minneapolis, Minn.: Dillon Press, 1981), p. 30.

6. Ibid., p. 58.

7. Judy Blume, *Otherwise Known as Sheila the Great* (New York: Dell Publishing Company, 1972), p. 111.

8. Judy Blume, *Letters to Judy* (New York: G.P. Putnam's Sons, 1986), p. 58.

9. Judy Blume, "Judy Blume's Books: Are You There, God? It's Me, Margaret," *JudyBlume.com*, n.d., <http://www.judyblume.com/margaret.html> (April 29, 2007).

10. Lee, p. 45.

11. Blume, *Letters to Judy*, p. 158.

12. Dick Gordon, "National Public Radio: The Connection," *TheConnection.org*, September 22, 2004, <http://www.theconnection.org/shows/2004/09/20040922_b_main.asp> (April 29, 2007).

13. Blume, Letters to Judy, pp. 27–28.

14. Ibid.

15. Leonard Marcus, *Author Talk: Conversations with Judy Blume, et al.* (New York: Simon & Schuster, 2000), p. 4.
16. Judy Blume, "Best Friends," *JudyBlume.com*, n.d., <http://www.judyblume.com/scrapbook.html> (April 29, 2007).
17. Lee, p. 63.
18. Marcus, p. 6.
19. "Autobiographical Statement," *Eighth Book of Junior Authors and Illustrators*, 2000, <http://www.edupaperback.org/showauth2.cfm?authid=15> (April 29, 2007).
20. Judy Blume, "Best Friends."
21. Lee, p. 70.
22. "Judy Blume's Interview Transcript," *Scholastic.com*, n.d., <http://content.scholastic.com/browse/collateral.jsp?id=10560_type=Contributor_typeId=1310> (April 29, 2007).
23. Lee, p. 73.
24. Gordon.

Chapter 4. From Dishes to "Dr. Suss"

1. "Autobiographical Statement," *Eighth Book of Junior Authors and Illustrators*, 2000, <http://www.edupaperback.org/showauth2.cfm?authid=15> (April 29, 2007).
2. Betsy Lee, *Judy Blume's Story* (Minneapolis, Minn.: Dillon Press, 1981), p. 75.
3. Cee Telford, *Judy Blume* (New York: Rosen Publishing Group: 2004), p. 25.
4. Lee, p. 74.
5. Ibid.
6. Telford, p. 25.
7. Lee, p. 77.

8. Judy Blume, *Letters to Judy* (New York: G.P. Putnam's Sons, 1986), pp. 131–132.

9. Ibid.

10. Lee, p. 52.

11. "A Wedding in Jerusalem: Spirituality in the Summertime," *UJC.org*, n.d., <http://www.ujc. org/content_display.html?ArticleID=10938> (April 29, 2007).

12. Judy Blume, "Best Friends," *JudyBlume.com*, n.d., <http://www.judyblume.com/scrapbook.html> (April 29, 2007).

13. Weidt, p. 14.

14. Ibid.

15. Lee, p. 91.

16. Dick Gordon, "National Public Radio: The Connection," *TheConnection.org*, September 22, 2004, <http://www.theconnection.org/shows/ 2004/09/20040922_b_main.asp> (April 29, 2007).

17. Linda Richards, "January Interview: Judy Blume," *January Magazine*, 2004, <http://www. januarymagazine.com/profiles/blume.html> (April 29, 2007).

18. Weidt, p. 10.

19. Lee, p. 92–93.

20. Justin Wintle and Emma Fisher, *The Pied Pipers* (New York: Paddington Press, 1975), p. 309.

21. Judy Blume, "Judy Blume Talks About Writing," *JudyBlume.com*, n.d., <http://www.judyblume. com/writing-jb.html> (April 29, 2007).

22. "Judy Blume's Interview Transcript," *Scholastic. com*, n.d., <http://content.scholastic.com/ browse/collateral.jsp?id=10560_type= Contributor_typeId=1310> (April 29, 2007).

23. "Author Chat with Judy Blume," *Teenlink.nypl.org*, November 19, 2002, <http://teenlink.nypl.org/blume_txt.html> (April 29, 2007).

24. Lee, p. 93.

25. Leonard Marcus, *Author Talk: Conversations with Judy Blume, et al.* (New York: Simon & Schuster, 2000), p. 6.

26. Christine Hill, *Ten Terrific Authors for Teens* (Berkeley Heights, N. J.: Enslow Publishers, Inc., 2000).

27. Judy Blume, "National Book Awards 2004 Acceptance Speech," *NationalBook.org*, November 17, 2004, <http://www.nationalbook.org/nbaacceptspeech_jblume04.html> (April 29, 2007).

28. "Author Chat with Judy Blume."

29. Judy Blume, "Judy's Anxiety Diary," *JudyBlume.com*, May 3, 1998, <http://www.judyblume.com/ss-diary1.html> (April 29, 2007).

30. Marcus, p. 6.

31. Weidt, p. 11.

32. Judy Blume, *Iggie's House* (New York: Bradbury Press, 1970), pp. 63–64.

33. Marcus, p. 7.

Chapter 5. A Writing Star Is Born

1. Judy Blume, *Places I Never Meant to Be* (New York: Simon & Schuster, 1999), p. 2.

2. Daniel Klein and Freke Vuijst, *The Half-Jewish Book: A Celebration* (New York: Villard Books, 2000), p. 32.

3. Ibid., p. 31.

4. Dick Gordon, "National Public Radio: The Connection," *TheConnection.org*, September 22, 2004, <http://www.theconnection.org/shows/2004/09/20040922_b_main.asp> (April 29, 2007).

5. RoseEtta Stone, "Interview with Judy Blume," *X-Rated Children's Books Newsletter*, October 18, 2002, <http://www.judyblume.com/articles/jrosettastone.html> (April 29, 2007).

6. Linda Richards, "January Interview: Judy Blume," *January Magazine*, 2004, <http://www.januarymagazine.com/profiles/blume.html> (April 29, 2007).

7. Gordon.

8. "Author Chat with Judy Blume," *Teenlink.nypl.org*, November 19, 2002, <http://teenlink.nypl.org/blume_txt.html> (April 29, 2007).

9. Judy Blume, "Judy Blume's Books: Tales of a Fourth Grade Nothing," *JudyBlume.com*, n.d., <http://www.judyblume.com/tales.html> (April 29, 2007).

10. Judy Blume, "Judy Blume's Books: The Pain and the Great One," *JudyBlume.com*, n.d., <http://www.judyblume.com/pain.html> (April 29, 2007).

11. Judy Blume, *Letters to Judy* (New York: G.P. Putnam's Sons, 1986), p. 91.

12. Betsy Lee, *Judy Blume's Story* (Minneapolis, Minn.: Dillon Press, 1981), p. 103.

13. Blume, *Letters to Judy*, p. 94.

14. Ibid., p. 100.

15. Judy Blume, "Judy Blume Talks About Writing," *JudyBlume.com*, n.d., <http://www.judyblume.com/writing-jb.html> (April 29, 2007).

16. Blume, Letters to Judy, p. 107.

17. Ibid., p. 63.

18. Lee, p. 105.

19. Julie Salamon, "Judy Blume, Girls' Friend, Makes a Move to the Movies," *The New York Times*, April 8, 2004, <http://www.judyblume.com/articles/NYT4-8-04(textonly).htm> (April 29, 2007).

20. Maryann Weidt, *Presenting Judy Blume* (New York: Dell Publishing, 1990), p. 125.

21. Judy Blume, "Judy Blume's Books: Tiger Eyes," *JudyBlume.com*, n.d., <http://www.judyblume.com/tiger.html> (April 29, 2007).

22. Weidt, p. 15.

23. Julie Salamon, "Judy Blume, Girls' Friend, Makes a Move to the Movies," *The New York Times*, April 8, 2004, <http://www.judyblume.com/articles/NYT4-8-04(textonly).htm> (April 29, 2007).

Chapter 6. A Voice for Females, Fighting to Be Heard

1. Judy Blume, *Deenie* (New York: Simon & Schuster, 1973), p. 103.

2. Justin Wintle and Emma Fisher, *The Pied Pipers* (New York: Paddington Press, 1975), p. 312.

3. Judy Blume, *Letters to Judy* (New York: G.P. Putnam's Sons, 1986), p. 83.

4. Dick Gordon, "National Public Radio: The Connection," *TheConnection.org*, September 22, 2004, <http://www.theconnection.org/shows/2004/09/20040922_b_main.asp> (April 29, 2007).

5. Judy Blume, "Judy Blume's Books: Deenie," *JudyBlume.com*, n.d., <http://www.judyblume.com/deenie.html> (April 29, 2007).

6. Blume, *Letters to Judy*, p. 45.

7. Judy Blume, *Blubber* (New York: Simon & Schuster, 1974), p. 129.

8. Ellen Barry, "Blume for President," *The Boston Phoenix*, May 21, 1998, <http://www.bostonphoenix.com/archive/features/98/05/21/JUDY_BLUME.html> (April 29, 2007).

9. "The 100 Most Frequently Challenged Books of 1990–1999," *ALA.org*, 2006, <http://www.ala.org/ala/oif/bannedbooksweek/bbwlinks/top100challenged.htm> (April 29, 2007).

10. Barry.

11. Wintle and Fisher, p. 314.

12. Alison Dorfman, "Bold Type: Alison Dorfman Interviews Judy Blume," *RandomHouse.com*, June 1998, <http://www.randomhouse.com/boldtype/0698/blume/interview.html> (April 29, 2007).

13. "Teen Spirit," *Guardian.co.uk*, 2005, <http://books.guardian.co.uk/departments/childrenandteens/story/0,6000,1500565,00.html> (April 29, 2007).

14. "Banned Books Awareness Message," *DeleteCensorship.org*, n.d., <http://www.deletecensorship.org/forever.html> (April 29, 2007).

15. Barry.

16. Blume, *Letters to Judy*, p. 175.

17. "Teen Spirit."

18. Linda Richards, "January Interview: Judy Blume," *January Magazine*, 2004, <http://www.januarymagazine.com/profiles/blume.html> (April 29, 2007).

19. Betsy Lee, *Judy Blume's Story* (Minneapolis, Minn.: Dillon Press, 1981), p. 110.

20. Judy Blume, *Places I Never Meant to Be* (New York: Simon & Schuster, 1999), p. 4.

21. Mark Oppenheimer, "Why Judy Blume Endures," *The New York Times*, November 16, 1997, <http://www.judyblume.com/articles/oppenheimer.html> (April 29, 2007).

22. Gordon.

23. Judy Blume, "Judy Blume Talks About Censorship," *JudyBlume.com*, n.d., <http://www.judyblume.com/censors.html> (April 29, 2007).

24. RoseEtta Stone, "Interview with Judy Blume," *X-Rated Children's Books Newsletter*, October 18, 2002, <http://www.judyblume.com/articles/jrosettastone.html> (April 29, 2007).

25. Ibid.

26. "American Library Association announces author Judy Blume ranks as second most censored author of past 15 years," *ALA.org*, September 21, 2004, <http://www.ala.org/ala/pr2004/september2004/Judyblume.htm> (April 29, 2007).

27. Oppenheimer.

Chapter 7. All in the Family

1. "All-Time Bestselling Children's Books," *PublishersWeekly.com*, December 17, 2001, <http://www.publishersweekly.com/index.asp?layout=article&articleid=CA187127> (April 29, 2007).

2. Maryann Weidt, *Presenting Judy Blume* (New York: Dell Publishing, 1990), p. 10.

3. Mark Oppenheimer, "Why Judy Blume Endures," *The New York Times*, November 16, 1997, <http://www.judyblume.com/articles/oppenheimer.html> (April 29, 2007).

4. Judy Blume, "Judy Blume's Books: Superfudge," *JudyBlume.com*, n.d., <http://www.judyblume. com/superfudge.html> (April 29, 2007).

5. Weidt, p. 23.

6. RoseEtta Stone, "Interview with Judy Blume," *X-Rated Children's Books Newsletter*, October 18, 2002, <http://www.judyblume.com/articles/ jrosettastone.html> (April 29, 2007).

7. Judy Blume, "Judy Blume's Books: Fudge-a-Mania," *JudyBlume.com*, n.d., <http://www.judyblume. com/fudge-a-mania.html> (April 29, 2007).

8. "Author Chat with Judy Blume," *Teenlink.nypl.org*, November 19, 2002, <http://teenlink.nypl.org/ blume_txt.html> (April 29, 2007).

9. Amanda Rogers, "Nine Reasons To Scoop Up Judy Blume's Tales of Fudge Hatcher," *Fort Worth Star-Telegram*, February 11, 2003.

10. Judy Blume, "Judy Blume's Books: Tales of a Fourth Grade Nothing," *JudyBlume.com*, n.d., <http://www.judyblume.com/tales.html> (April 29, 2007).

11. Linda Richards, "January Interview: Judy Blume," *January Magazine*, 2004, <http://www. januarymagazine.com/profiles/blume.html> (April 29, 2007).

12. Julie Salamon, "Judy Blume, Girls' Friend, Makes a Move to the Movies," *The New York Times*, April 8, 2004, <http://www.judyblume.com/ articles/NYT4-8-04(textonly).htm> (April 29, 2007).

13. Judy Blume, *Letters to Judy* (New York: G.P. Putnam's Sons, 1986), p. 14.

14. Don Swaim, "Audio Interview with Judy Blume," CBS Radio, 1986.

15. Ibid.

16. Ibid.

17. Judy Blume, "Judy Blume's Books: Just as Long as We're Together," *JudyBlume.com*, n.d., <http://www.judyblume.com/just_as.html> (April 29, 2007).

18. Weidt, p. 26.

19. "Judy Blume's Interview Transcript," *Scholastic.com*, n.d., <http://content.scholastic.com/browse/collateral.jsp?id=10560_type=Contributor_typeId=1310> (April 29, 2007).

20. Judy Blume, "Judy Blume's Books: Here's to You, Rachel Robinson," *JudyBlume.com*, n.d., <http://www.judyblume.com/rachel.html> (April 29, 2007).

21. Ray Suarez, "Talk of the Nation," *National Public Radio*, December 24, 1998.

Chapter 8. Endless Summers

1. Judy Blume, "Judy Talks About Summer Sisters: The Background," *JudyBlume.com*, n.d., <http://www.judyblume.com/ss-backgrnd.html> (April 29, 2007).

2. Judy Blume, "National Book Awards 2004 Acceptance Speech," *NationalBook.org*, November 17, 2004, <http://www.nationalbook.org/nbaacceptspeech_jblume04.html> (April 29, 2007).

3. Jennifer Frey, "Fiction Heroine," *The Washington Post*, November 17, 2004, <http://www.washingtonpost.com/wp-dyn/articles/A55767-2004Nov16.html> (April 29, 2007).

4. Joseph P. Kahn, "Judy Blume's Summer Camp: The Controversial Queen of Kid Lit Beats the Heat at the Vineyard," *Boston Globe*, July 6, 1995.

5. Judy Blume, *Letters to Judy* (New York: G.P. Putnam's Sons, 1986), p. 127.

6. Ibid., p. 126.

7. Maryann Weidt, *Presenting Judy Blume* (New York: Dell Publishing, 1990), p. 16.

8. Blume, "Judy Talks About Summer Sisters: The Background."

9. Ibid.

10. Judy Blume, "Judy Blume's Books: Fudge-a-Mania," *JudyBlume.com*, n.d., <http://www.judyblume. com/fudge-a-mania.html> (April 29, 2007).

11. Blume, "Judy Talks About Summer Sisters: The Background."

12. Leonard Marcus, *Author Talk: Conversations with Judy Blume, et al*. (New York: Simon & Schuster, 2000), p. 7.

13. Don Swaim, "Audio Interview with Judy Blume," CBS Radio, 1986.

14. Cynthia Leitich Smith, "Interview with Judy Blume," *CynthiaLeitichSmith.com*, 2002, <http://www.cynthialeitichsmith.com/lit_ resources/authors/interviews/JudyBlume.html> (April 29, 2007).

15. Ibid.

16. RoseEtta Stone, "Interview with Judy Blume," *X-Rated Children's Books Newsletter*, October 18, 2002, <http://www.judyblume.com/articles/ jrosettastone.html> (April 29, 2007).

17. Justin Wintle and Emma Fisher, *The Pied Pipers* (New York: Paddington Press, 1975), pp. 311–312.

18. Judy Blume, "What's Up with Judy," *JudyBlume. com*, n.d., <http://www.judyblume.com/ whats_up.html> (April 29, 2007).

Chapter 9. With Risk Comes Reward

1. Judy Blume, "Judy Blume's Books: The Pain and the Great One," *JudyBlume.com*, n.d., <http://www.judyblume.com/pain.html> (April 29, 2007).

2. "Teen Spirit," *Guardian.co.uk*, 2005, <http://books.guardian.co.uk/departments/childrenandteens/story/0,6000,1500565,00.html> (April 29, 2007).

3. Ellen Barry, "Blume for President," *The Boston Phoenix*, May 21, 1998, <http://www.bostonphoenix.com/archive/features/98/05/21/JUDY_BLUME.html> (April 29, 2007).

4. Ray Suarez, "Talk of the Nation," *National Public Radio*, December 24, 1998.

5. Barry.

6. "Author Chat with Judy Blume," *Teenlink.nypl.org*, November 19, 2002, <http://teenlink.nypl.org/blume_txt.html> (April 29, 2007).

7. "The 100 Most Frequently Challenged Books of 1990–1999," *ALA.org*, 2006, <http://www.ala.org/ala/oif/bannedbooksweek/bbwlinks/top100challenged.htm> (April 29, 2007).

8. Justin Wintle and Emma Fisher, *The Pied Pipers* (New York: Paddington Press, 1975), p. 315.

9. "Margaret Edwards Award," *ALA.org*, n.d., <http://www.ala.org/ala/yalsa/booklistsawards/margaretaedwards/margaretedwards.htm> (April 29, 2007).

10. Judy Blume, "National Book Awards 2004 Acceptance Speech," *NationalBook.org*, November 17, 2004, <http://www.national-book.org/nbaacceptspeech_jblume04.html> (April 29, 2007).

11. Jill Lopresti, "Puberty Unfolds in the Name of Judy Blume at the Annoyance Theatre," *Columbia Chronicle Online*, March 15, 1999, <http://www.columbiachronicle.com/back/1999_spring/99mar15/ae2.html> (April 29, 2007).

12. Jennifer Frey, "Fiction Heroine," *The Washington Post*, November 17, 2004, <http://www.washingtonpost.com/wp-dyn/articles/A55767-2004Nov16.html> (April 29, 2007).

13. Judy Blume, "What's Up with Judy," *JudyBlume.com*, n.d., <http://www.judyblume.com/whats_up.html> (April 29, 2007).

14. "Spotlight On . . . Judy Blume," *RandomHouse.com*, 2004, <http://www.randomhouse.com/teachers/authors/results.pperl?authorid=2611> (April 29, 2007).

15. Linda Richards, "January Interview: Judy Blume," *January Magazine*, 2004, <http://www.januarymagazine.com/profiles/blume.html> (April 29, 2007).

16. Judy Blume, "What's Up with Judy."

17. Mark Oppenheimer, "Why Judy Blume Endures," *The New York Times*, November 16, 1997, <http://www.judyblume.com/articles/oppenheimer.html> (April 29, 2007).

18. Dick Gordon, "National Public Radio: The Connection," *TheConnection.org*, September 22, 2004, <http://www.theconnection.org/shows/2004/09/20040922_b_main.asp> (April 29, 2007).

In Her Own Words

1. Judy Blume, *Letters to Judy* (New York: G.P. Putnam's Sons, 1986), p. 135.

2. Ibid., p. 62.

3. Ibid., p. 171.

4. Sybil Steinberg, "PW Interviews: Judy Blume," *Publisher's Weekly*, April 17, 1978.

5. Justin Wintle and Emma Fisher, *The Pied Pipers* (New York: Paddington Press, 1975), p. 312.

6. Ibid, p. 320.

7. Blume, Letters to Judy, p. 12.

8. "Author Chat with Judy Blume," *Teenlink.nypl.org*, November 19, 2002, <http://teenlink.nypl.org/blume_txt.html> (April 29, 2007).

9. Leonard Marcus, *Author Talk: Conversations with Judy Blume, et al.* (New York: Simon & Schuster, 2000), p. 8.

10. Anna Bondoc and Meg Daly, *Letters of Intent* (New York: The Free Press, 1999), p. 206.

11. "Judy Blume's Interview Transcript," *Scholastic.com*, n.d., <http://content.scholastic.com/browse/collateral.jsp?id=10560_type=Contributor_typeId=1310> (April 29, 2007).

12. RoseEtta Stone, "Interview with Judy Blume," *X-Rated Children's Books Newsletter*, October 18, 2002, <http://www.judyblume.com/articles/jrosettastone.html> (April 29, 2007).

13. Ibid.

14. "All Things Considered," *National Public Radio*, September 15, 2004, <http://www.npr.org/templates/story/story.php?storyId=3919695> (April 29, 2007).

15. Judy Blume, "Is Harry Potter Evil?" *The New York Times*, October 22, 1999, <http://www.judyblume.com/articles/harry_potter_oped.html> (April 29, 2007).

Glossary

acclaim—A high form of praise.

catharsis—An emotional release; the opportunity to let go of built-up tension.

dinghy—A small rowboat.

façade—Someone's (or something's) outer appearance.

fruitless—Unsuccessful or yielding poor results.

galleys—An early product of the book publishing process used to make corrections before printing the final pages.

genesis—A beginning.

incensed—Angry.

monogamous—Being in an exclusive sexual relationship with just one person.

mononucleosis—A highly contagious disease.

protagonist—The main character driving a plot.

rites of passage—An important event that marks a person's transition into a new stage of life.

scoliosis—The curving of the spine.

serendipity—Good fortune.

serial—A story that is run in several installments.

Further Reading

Books

Ludwig, Elisa. *Who Wrote That? Judy Blume.* Broomall, Pa.: Chelsea House Publishers, 2004.

Telford, Cee. *Judy Blume.* New York: Rosen Publishing Group, 2004.

Tracy, Kathleen. *Classic Storytellers: Judy Blume.* Bear, Del.: Mitchell Lane Publishers, 2005.

Internet Addresses

Judy Blume's Web site
http://www.judyblume.com

Judy Blume Bibliography
http://www.carr.org/mae/blume/blum-bks.htm

Index